Only For Your Happy Life

Hiranya Borah

First Published in October 2022

ISBN: 978-93-5668-615-1

BLUEROSE PUBLISHERS

www.BlueRoseONE.com

info@bluerosepublishers.com

+91 8882 898 898

Cover Design:

Aman Sharma

Typographic Design:

Namrata Saini

Distributed by: BlueRose, Amazon, Flipkart

Preface

The articles do not carry any new thoughts nor give any new philosophy towards life. Underlying philosophy of the articles are like new packaging by small grocers, from big packets bought from large farms/ whole sellers. Readers will not find anything new philosophy in it. Some of the stories and sub-stories are written in lighter vein and not to hurt sentiments of the involved persons. The stories are independent of each other and based on my own experiences, real experiences encountered by my friends which are however, laced with some fictional thoughts. They are not arranged in a particular order and placed randomly.

I changed the names of the persons involved in different stories to safeguard their privacy whenever the stories shared here are not directly involving me and my core family members.

I am always thankful to my readers for their encouragement in my literary life.

Hiranya Borah

Contents

Chapter: 1

On Saying 'I Love You'

Let me ask all my friends, 'How many of you actually used these three magical words, I love you, to someone you love?'

I am not asking how many of you have told these words to your GF/BF/children/spouse, I am asking how many of you have told these magical words to your old parents/grandparents/uncles/aunts/old servants recently.

Probably, a very few of you have told these words in the last 24 hours to any of the persons in the group stated above. Some more will be added in the list if time period is extended to one month.

Many of us probably ceased to think that those people are in the list of our love ones. I am not blaming any one of you. I am only trying to share some of my own experiences on this issue.

I hugged my father for the last time in 1989 when my son was born. My father died in 1997. That means, I did not hug him for the last 8 years of his life. Now, whenever, my son/daughter hugs me, I feel very happy and also feel a pain in the bosom of my heart thinking what I had deprived my father few happy moments for the last 8 years of his life before his death.

For the last time, I put my arms around my mother in March, 2005 when she was critically ill. Unfortunately, I could not even put my head down on her lap when she died in May, 2005 as I could not reach my village before her cremation.

But I still vividly remember the last hug I made to her. She pressed her chest to my face and did not allow me to take my face away for long five minutes or so. At the time of her death, none of us (including my brother and sister) was present beside her. She fought her last battle of life all alone. We justify our actions with some good or bad reasons. However, at the back of the mind, I always think, she would have survived few more months had I been with her.

Why I am writing this now after so many years? Because I realize now, I had missed an opportunity to make my parents happier.

Please, please do not miss the opportunity to tell 'Hey, old buddy/old sweetheart, I love you, I care for you' to your close elderly people, before it is too late to realize what you are going to miss in your life forever.

Chapter: 2

Happiness is only a phone call away

All of us are experienced, at least once in a month, waiting anxiously for a phone call from someone, may be, for different reasons. We always see the mobile phone, again and again, thinking, why it is not ringing or whether I have missed the call by not hearing the sound of the ring. We use to check the apparatus whether it is ok or not. Finally, when we get the call, we are very happy and relaxed or may feel something.

However, all those activities what we are doing, knowing well that the phone call will come only when the caller will make the call. The caller will decide when to call to the person who is anxiously waiting for the call. The receiver has no control over it.

Sometimes, we think, we shall not receive the call to show our unhappiness/annoyance for the late call- but finally we pick up the call at once, knowing that we want to receive the call more than the caller, who happens to be the decision maker.

All parents of my age (50 plus), experience many times the anxiety of not picking up phones by our children despite of repeated phone calls. Sometimes, you may have to call his/her friends/colleagues to know about his/her wellbeing. After, calling to his/her friends, you may sometimes get a good verbal thrashing from your ward. But most of you might be doing the same mistake again and again to ease out your anxiety.

But your wards, are cool with the following probable answers: i) I forgot to carry the phone to the college/ party; ii) lack of charge in battery of the mobile; iii) I was in a meeting and so on. Despite of the verbal thrashing or the apparent lie on their part, once you got the phone call, you become very happy and relaxed.

Now, consider the people, who are around 20 year's senior to us in age (70 plus). They also want to hear from us, something on regular basis. On the other hand we may be extremely busy (at least mentally) with our routine duties including calling our children in time, attending phone calls from our boss/ client/ colleague/ spouse/ GF/BF.

Let us ask this question to ourselves, 'Can we not spare two minutes a day to call our parents and other elderly ones who are waiting for our calls every day looking at the mobile/land line phone from morning to till midnight and even getting up from sleep in the early morning to check the phone whether phone is properly placed or working properly so that any call from you is not missed?'

Probably many of us are not mentally prepared to spare those two minutes a day. But, yes we can do it with some planning. Fix a time, may be after your dinner, to call your elderly near and dear ones, every day. Once you are accustomed with the timing, you are unlikely to forget to call him/her.

My humble submission is to all of those who are not calling their elderly dear ones, please spare two minutes and make them happier so that he/she can also boast to his friends/relatives that my son/ daughter/ nephew/ niece telephones me every day. Your little effort and small spending on telephone will make your near and dear ones happier, which in turn make you also happier day by day.

Chapter: 3

Try to smile when you are even in pain

Earlier it was boasted that only human being can smile and that is why it is precious. But now scientists find that even animals and plants can smile when they are happy. Smile is always contiguous like any other moods of any living being. You always try to see smiles on the faces of your love ones. Even when you are in trouble/pain you perhaps try to be in good mood in front of your love ones so that they are not unduly worried about your wellbeing.

But can we smile to a stranger? We advise our young ones not to mingle or not be very friendly to unknown persons. In public places like metro stations, through public announcement systems also, we normally hear that 'Do not be friendly to the strangers'.

These types of announcement/ cautions are necessary, considering the law and order situation in the entire world. But, if we close all the doors for all the strangers, we shall close doors for development of new friendship as well. Probably, that will be contrary to our earlier teachings to make friend all over the world. Personally, I make lot of new friends (you may call them as new acquaintances only) during the last few years who happened to be totally strangers to me and interestingly nobody had introduced me to them and vice versa. I proudly say that some of them are now good friends of mine and glad to inform you that they are from across the globe. However, one common observation I had made in all of them, all of them have smiling faces.

Is smile so important in life? Is smiling face is an indication of timidity? Is it deceptive for others whom he/she wants to flinch? All these questions are coming out of our own experiences. As the answers are also coming out of our own experiences, we have to deal with all these smiling faces differently.

An innocent smile of a toddler can make you happy at any time. However, we must admit, every smile sends you a different messages, if it emanates from different personalities. Even for the same person, context of smile may be different. A lion, may also smile, when a zebra is approaching to its striking distance. Same lion may also smile when he is approached by his cubs or when a lioness approaches him for enticing to have sex. Even it is said about some bosses, 'Today boss is smiling and therefore grave danger is looming ahead of us'.

When and why we are worried to see smiles on some persons' faces- I need not have to explain. As our mythology says 'Smile of Mahakaal (God of death) is the most dangerous indication for any living being as that is the last smile- one is destined to see.'

How do you feel about a plastic smile? When an airhostess welcomes you into her aircraft or a model on the ramp appears with a smile, nobody finds any warmth in it. But when you see a similar smile from a neighbor, your mercury level may shoot up in excitement, depending upon his/her relations with you and depending upon his/her earlier records. For example, if he/she asks for a favour after every smile, you will be worried and on the other hand, if he/she gives a lift, you will be more than happy.

Unfortunately, smile on the others face cannot be controlled by you. So keep smiling always! Let the other person interpret your smile!

This article is dedicated to one of my maternal aunts who just one hour before her death at around 6 in the morning told me with a sweet smile, 'Go home my child, take bath, take breakfast and take a nap before coming to hospital again to meet me'.

Chapter: 4

Learn to hear a 'No'... While Saying 'I love you'

In 2014 a highly educated boy of a very reputed university attacked a lady classmate with sharp weapons who curtly refused his proposal to love him. He also committed suicide after committing the heinous crime. However, this is not a 'one off example' of such crimes committed by jilted lovers.

Every day, it is happening all over the world. Every day, one spurned lover either throws acid on the face of lady or stabs her whom he claims to love from the core of his heart. As per statistics provided by the National Crime Records Bureau (NCRB), Ministry of Home Affairs, Government of India, in 2012, there were 24923 rape cases, 45351 cases of Assault on women with intent to outrage her modesty and 9173 cases of insult to modesty of woman. These were only recorded cases against women. There might be lot of unrecorded cases where women were in the receiving ends.

Why women are targeted? Why a spurned lover attacks a lady whom he apparently loves? These are generic questions. But let us concentrate on those cases where spurned lovers attack their loved ones. The moot question, can anybody harm a person whom he/she actually loves? Perhaps, that is not possible. Then, can we call it as an aberration to drive a divine activity to a heinous crime? Perhaps yes, that may be one of the plausible answers.

Before going to a serious discussion on the issue, let me introduce a friend who looks at 'love' in his own perspective. During our college days, as per his own claim, he proposed, each and every beautiful girl of our class. In his own words, none of our classmates had accepted his proposal. But all the girls, now all are middle aged women are good friends of him. According to him, to love somebody was his prerogative, whereas acceptance or rejection was her (their) prerogative. He claims that even now he proposes beautiful girls/women, with the same result; a rejection on his faces. However, in the process he made a big pool of beautiful girls/women as his good friends. His wife is also pretty confident that none of the female friends will ever be GF of her husband. As far my information, none of his women friends have any grudge against him for proposing the other women as well or even their husbands have any bad feeling about him. As per his claim which I also endorse, he has lot of respect for all those ladies whom he once proposed and also respect for their decisions to reject his proposals. When someone asked, had any of them accepted his proposal, would he stopped proposing another one, his answer was an emphatic 'No'.

Now let us come to the serious part of the problem. While a man proposes a girl/ woman whom he loves, he has to muster a lot of courage- (assuming that girls/women normally will not propose a man). But only a brave man has the courage to hear a 'no' and respect the decision of the girl/woman whom he loves. A brave man will never hurt the sentiment of the girl/woman and he will always be helpful to the girl/woman knowing fully well that she will never be with him or she will never love him.

In this world, unfortunately, there are very few extremely brave people like Temucin, Bidhan Chandra Roy who can digest the rejection of someone whom they actually love, and made those painful moments to build inner strength to do something exceptional for their community/country/race or as a whole for the mankind.

Though everyone cannot be like those well-known personalities of history, there may be many unsung heroes in different fields, about whom we may know very little or nothing at all. However, they are also hero of their own right. Similarly there may be thousand brave persons after getting a rejection, they may excel in one field or other field(s) which may be unknown to others. Those brave persons may also be happy with their life partners and also faithful to them throughout their lives. They may not shed tears whole of their lives for the girl once he used to love.

On the other hand, what a coward will do after getting a rejection from a lady whom he thinks, he loves? He may put himself in to a cocoon, which he will make to destroy himself. Alternatively, he may physically or mentally or socially harm the lady whom he claims to love. Unfortunately, there will be many more cowards compared to the number of brave people. That is why crime graph against women are going northwards.

Coming to our own country, it is a fact that most of the Indian families do not discuss about personal life of self or about their children amongst themselves. To be more precise, we do not share our experiences- bad or good with our children to avoid embarrassments- if any; forget about discussing about love affairs etc.

However, now it is felt that time has come, at least we should realize that we all have the social obligation to teach our children in general, and sons, in particular to be brave enough to muster the courage to hear a 'No' not only in the fields of education/ job market but also in the delicate world of 'love'. They should be taught that loving someone may be their decisions but to be loved by someone, is the decision of someone else. They should be taught to respect others' decisions and take those decisions with humility. They should be taught that every one may not get back equal love from the other party. Even he/she who has rejected you, may be in the same position where you are at this juncture (they may also be spurned by others!)! Therefore, there is no embarrassment for a refusal from someone you love, nor, it will demean your masculinity/ personality/ or your position in the society.

So be brave, take a 'No' into your own stride and look for a new friend. Who knows, the new friend may accept your proposal and God wishes, she may be qualitatively far better than the one, who had rejected you.

As mature persons we may also teach our daughters how to react to an unwanted proposal to avoid confrontation. A girl also should respect the sentiment of a person who proposes to her. One should remember that, success of a person depends upon the articulation of words of a person to say a 'No' to a proposal. How to say a 'no' depends upon the situation under what condition, you have to say a 'No'. Keeping the central theme of a 'No', you may convey the message without actually pronouncing the word 'No'. Sometimes you may have to say an empathic 'No' and sometimes a very apologetic 'No'. For example, you may have to say a 'No' to a weak limpet very strongly when his proposal is not acceptable to you. But when the person is your boss (or someone, very powerful) proposes, you may not be that straight forward. But you must have to convey the message that you are not going to accept his proposal, if you are not interested. Remember, saying 'yes' is the easiest answer anybody can give. Fulfillment of the promise is, however, another matter. Sometimes, a 'no' may cost thousands of lives. Best example is perhaps 'Destruction of Spanish Armada' in the eighteen Century when Queen Elizabeth refused the marriage proposal of Spanish King. Therefore, while saying a 'No', sometimes, you have to be very cautious/ diplomatic, as this may jeopardize your own or your family's security in terms of physical or financial or may be in both. In many occasions, we have to say a 'Yes' instead of a 'No' to quell over an impending storm.

Here, I am not suggesting any specific answer for saying a 'no' to a 'love proposal', but I am just saying, keeping the central theme of a 'strong no' intact, one should be polite and impress the other party to see a reason in it.

So we have to teach our ward(s), particularly to our sons, to be brave to accept a 'No' into their own strides and look for new willing girlfriends.

Chapter: 5

How to say a 'NO'

There is a reference in the famous book 'The God Father- Part-I' of Mario Puzo on saying a 'No' to a proposal. Sometimes you may have to say an empathic 'No' and sometimes a very apologetic 'No'. For example, you may have to say a 'No' to your children very strongly when their demands are not reasonable. But when your boss (or someone, very powerful) asks something/ unreasonable favour from you, you may not be that straight forward. But you must have to convey the message that you are not going to fulfill his/her unreasonable demand(s). Please always remember, saying 'yes' is the easiest answer anybody can give.

Sometimes, a 'no' may cost thousands of lives, best example is as stated above, Destruction of Spanish Armada. Therefore, while saying a 'No' sometimes you have to be very cautious/diplomatic, as this may jeopardize your/your family's security. In many occasions, we have to say 'Yes' instead of a 'No' to quell over an impending storm. Sometimes, you cannot reject a foolish suggestion of your boss/ friend/well-wisher, because you think that, you may lose goodwill/a friend/ a well-wisher by just saying a 'No'. Sometimes you do not say 'No' at a particular moment, as at that time you want to avoid an argument due to some reasons.

But some persons have a habit to start any sentence by saying a "No'. For example, if you ask him/her when he is returning from the market, (you know the fact), 'Are you returning from the market? His answer would be, 'No, I am returning from the market.' Those persons are known for their negativity. For them saying a 'No' is not difficult. But to mean it- sometimes for them also, it may be very difficult to say a 'no'.

If you muster the art of saying a 'No' when you actually mean it, you will be definitely a successful person.

A few instances when a subordinate says a 'no' to his/her boss by saying:

1. Very good proposal sir (for a very stupid proposal/ to do something against rule), but I have an alternative submission which may serve your purpose (it will benefit you), within the rules, as well as, it may enhance your reputation before ---sir (his /her boss). (A good one)

2. It will be against the existing rule. / It will not give any desired result. / It will not help our organization. (A very bad one-it may invite trouble). To make a little bit tolerable by your boss, you may replace 'will' by, 'may be.'

3. It is a very good proposal, but sir, as you know, our (including yours) boss is very negative towards good proposals coming from intelligent (sic!) his/ her subordinates like us. (Stumped- but invite no trouble)

4. I shall submit a draft proposal as soon as possible, as advised by you.(you submit a proposal just opposite to what he/she had advised-may be, in consultation with your super boss).(Result awaited)

5. Extremely good proposal sir. But I think, this proposal should be initiated by the other section! (Good answer. But still you may invite trouble, if your boss insists).

6. Do you think I am a fool, to initiate such a stupid proposal? I may also inform -- (his/her boss) about this. (It is very bad answer. However, it may not invite trouble immediately, as it appears, you have a good rapport with your super boss).

7. I am not getting any headway, sir/Madam. Kindly guide me sir/madam. (If you start with 'As discussed, ---,' your boss will never sign under your note, the file may remain on Boss's table forever!)

And so on...........

And finally, the best one may be,

I AM DOING IT SIR/MADAM. (IT WILL NEVER BE COMPLETED/ SUBMITTTED SO LONG EITHER OF YOU ARE TRANSFERRED FROM THAT SECTION/ DEPARTMENT)

A few instances when a beautiful damsel says a 'no' to a proposal by saying:

1. Sorry man, I am already engaged. You are late by a whisker. (Good one)

2. Have you ever seen your face on a mirror? (It is a very bad one-it may invite trouble)

3. I love you always like my own brother. (Stumped-but invite no trouble)

4. I would have said yes, had the proposal come from your brother/ your best friend. (Since his brother/ his best friend is better off-it may invite trouble)

5. Thank you. I am delighted. But right now, I am concentrating in my studies/ career. (Good answer. But still it may invite stalking/ persuasion).

6. Do you know whom you are talking? (Very bad answer. It may not invite trouble as your brother/father is powerful enough to do the needful.)

And so on...........

And finally,

I AM TOTALLY PUZZLED. I NEED SOME MORE TIME TO THINK OVER IT. (I am sure you will ensure, that particular magic moment will never come).

Chapter: 6

Good Morning Sir/Madam and everybody

Never ever force anybody to address you sir, if he or she does not want to address you sir. Why I am saying this? Please read this story. I am sure why I am saying so, you are intelligent enough to understand.

Mr. X, Y and Z were three batch mates of a reputed company and joined their company on the same day. However, on the basis of the first interview, Mr. X became the senior most at the time of posting. In due course of time, they became good friends. Life was going on as usual for all the three friends for the next twenty years.

Among the three, Mr. X was extremely vocal in airing his views which sometimes made him unpopular among the seniors despite of his intelligence and workaholic nature. However, he was extremely popular among the juniors for his helping attitude and timely advices whenever they approach him to solve both official and personal problems.

For airing his views for the right cause made him so un-popular among the seniors, after twenty years of service, Mr. X failed to get a regular promotion whereas both Mr. Y and Z got their promotions superseding Mr. X.

After that promotion, friendship between Mr. X and Y remained same but Mr. Z, who happened to be the junior-most among them prior to the last promotion behaved differently. After his promotion, he stopped any non-official and non-formal meeting with Mr. X.

Finally, one day Mr. Z conveyed to Mr. X through a much junior officer that Mr. X should show respect to Mr. Z as his senior then onwards at any formal official meeting.

Mr. X got the message and followed Mr. Z's order in letter and spirit. How?

He started to show proper respect (?) to Mr. Z at any place at any time. Whenever Mr. X met Mr. Z, he immediately used to stand up from the Chair, bow him and wish him 'Good morning/ good afternoon/ etc. Sir.'

Mr. Z became very happy thinking that he was able to show one of the most arrogant officers his proper place. He enjoyed every bit of time he spent with Mr. X. Mr. X's good morning and good afternoon had so much soothing effect on him that, he used to look forward his meeting with Mr. X on any official forum. His (Mr. X's) yes sir, yes sir became a music to his ears in any formal meeting. During that period, Mr. Z used to relish his position like never before.

One fine morning, Mr. X and Y were discussing some personal matters in Mr. Y's chamber. During that time, Mr. Z also made a crash door entry to Mr. Y's chamber.

Mr. X stood up immediately, bowed to him and said, 'Good morning Sir.'

Mr. Y was surprised to see his funny style of saying good morning to a friend of twenty odd years. Mr. Y asked Mr. X, 'Why you are behaving like this, you ba--d?'

Mr. X smiled sarcastically and replied, "Nowadays, I say -'Good Morning Sir' to everybody; even to the street dogs, as I do not know when and how one will bite (me) from behind. Nowadays, I have a feeling that everyone holding some power can backstab me. That is why I respect all the seniors and powerful by licking their feet. Nobody looks at company's interest. Everybody counts how many times your junior says, 'Good morning your highness.' Now I also become very intelligent."

Mr. Z felt a pain of a strong virtual slap on his face.

To add salt to his (Mr. Z) injury (hurting ego), Mr. X told Mr. Y, 'Whenever any dog in the street forced me to show respect, fearing an impending bite, I always show respect to him as per the way he desires. When I utter good morning, I actually mean, you ba—d you deserve a kick on your butt, but alas I have to say good morning to a ba—d who may not know even who was his father.'

With a pause he said again, 'However, when I say good morning to Mr. Z, I actually mean it. After all, I always show my sincere respect to all the deserving persons irrespective of what they demand and what they deserve.'

Mr. Z could not find appropriate words to counter the remarks of Mr. X. Only he could manage a smile on a crying face.

Now you also understand why Mr. X did not get his promotion in time!

However, the bottom lines are:

Always remember that every 'good morning' is not necessarily as good as it sounds! Every good morning may mean 'go to hell, you ba–d'. Therefore never force anyone to say 'good morning' against his or her will. After all, indifference attitude of a person is always better than the hidden curse, coated with a 'good morning sir'. Always remember if you deserve a 'good morning sir/ madam' from anyone, you will definitely get it with or without any demand from your side. Always respect the will of the other person irrespective of his seniority and social standing compared to you.

Chapter: 7

On Being Human

When I was in Class-XI (Pre-University) in 1976-77, Cotton College, a lady teacher asked all the students one by one what we would like to be (aim in life). Many of my classmates gave answers like, 'I want to be an IAS officer to serve the country.' Many wanted to be Engineers or Professors etc. As it was a statistics class, so no one wanted to be a doctor! When my turn came, I answered, 'I want to be a human being.'

Everybody in the class laughed and one of my friends, who is now a very big boss of a reputed company, commented, 'Hiranya, are you a monkey now?'

I replied back, 'I do not know.'

Till now I am asking myself the same question, 'Am I able to become a human being?' However, nowadays, I have seen many youngsters are using T-shirt with an imprint 'Being Human'.

I am happy that at least somebody has realized-what I meant to say in 1976-77.

Few years ago, I was sitting with one of the senior most officers of our Ministry and requesting him to do a favour to some of us (a group of officers who were similarly placed). His driver, who was also present at that time, all of a sudden, requested our boss, 'Sir, help him as far as possible, because, he is a god-like man. If you help him, God will definitely help you, sir.'

Afterwards, I asked the driver why he had said so. He replied, 'Sir, we have seen lots of officers who are queuing up to donate blood to the boss or his/her relatives. But we saw you the only officer, who wanted to donate blood to a daughter of a group D staff.'

I did not say anything to him. It reminded me one of the most important incidents of my life- I could not attend last few days of my mother who was on her death bed during 2005. Therefore, I had to ask again myself the same question, 'Am I human being? Forget about the demigod status as bestowed upon me by the driver!'

In my assessment, our misdeeds may be much heavier than the one or two good things; we used to do during our life time. We may have more vices than good habits. Mostly, we boast our vices as our heroic activities. Knowingly or unknowingly, we may have done more harm to humanity than good things for the society, which are the main obstacles for a person to become a 'human being'.

One of our relatives once said, 'You are a very successful father and a successful husband. You have done so much for them. Your children and your wife should be thankful to you, whatever you have done for them.'

I simply replied, 'Better you ask them about their comments on your observations on these issues.'

I know that, like most of the spouses, my wife also, during her outburst, used to say, I have spoiled her life/career. Occasionally, like most of the children, my children also compare with some more successful fathers. After all we are living in a comparative world!

We always, pat our backs for any small good thing we have done for others and always justify our misdeeds with strong arguments. I am no exception to that.

I think, to become a god is easier than to become a human being. Sometime I extend my helping hand to the needy. But in the next moment I ask myself whether I did it for nothing or to satisfy my own ego? I always ask this question to myself after doing a 'good deed' without a concrete answer.

During my hostel life in college days, I along with some of our classmates used to stay overnight with our hostel-mates who were hospitalized for some illness. Still, I am not sure, whether I helped them or I just want to avoid my studies and running away from my studies with a justification which appears to be a noble cause in the eyes of others.

My above activity can be seen two completely diametrically opposite perspectives. One- I extended my helping hand to a hostel mate when he needed it most. Therefore, I did a good job and I can pat on my back. Second perspective is completely opposite to that. My parents sent me to the hostel with their hard earned money to study so that I could have gotten a better job. But what I was doing! I spent whole night without any sleep and thus putting pressure on my health and study at the cost of a hostel mate, who after his release from the hospital, gave a mere 'thank you'. Can I justify my wasting of time if I consider the hope of my parents placed on my shoulders? So while doing something good to someone, I was probably doing injustice to my parents. Actually where I was standing? Can anybody enlighten me on this account? On being human, I find lots of difficulties in these types of balancing acts.

You may find some very good persons who have done lot of good things for the society. But ask their near and dear ones about them, they may have diametrically opposite opinions about them. There is a proverb, 'Charity begins at home.' If we have to follow that principle, then those persons (socially highly appreciated persons) may not get good marks- some may not get even pass marks as a 'human being'.

In a charted bus, in 1995, I have an argument with an elderly lady when she claimed that she had never indulged in any corrupt practices in her entire life. I asked her one simple question, 'Madam, when do you come to office and when do you leave?'

She replied, 'I reach always office by 10 O'clock and leave by 5 PM.'

'What is your office timing?'

'9AM to 5-30 PM.'

'That means, you are getting extra salary for 1-30 hours daily which is almost 20% of the working hours for which you are paid by the Government. And if we count for entire month it is about 30-36 hours. For the whole year, it is 400 hours and for whole service life (about 35 years) it is whopping 14000 hours. If you are given even Rs.100 for each hour work/available for work, then you are getting roughly Rs.14, 00,000/- without doing any official work. If you put in recurring deposit scheme, it will be more than Rs.50-60 lakhs. Is it not a massive corruption you are indulging?'(Figures are given as per salary structure at that time).

'Everybody is doing that.'

'That is true, but that will not make you a spotless person.'

Should I request my National Accounts Division, CSO to estimate this amount for entire country since independence? It may exceed the largest scam amount of the whole world- let alone India. Are we not part and parcel of this organized loot?

Why I am telling this? Because, we cannot see our face; we can see only the image of our face in a mirror. Similarly we cannot see our own personality by ourselves; we can see our personality through the reflection from the society towards us.

It may also so happen, one tells you in the morning that you are like a god and in the same evening somebody else can say you that, you are no less than a devil. Nobody will say you in the whole day, that 'You are a 'human being'. That is why I wonder when I shall be a 'human being'.

Even for the same action, you may get kudos and brickbats from the same persons after a period time. One of the best example is (somewhere I read or somebody told me) about a Japanese spy, who was condemned to death for passing information to the Allied forces. Whole family was subjected for all humiliations for his unpatriotic action. But after few days of his death, he became a National hero as he was doing all the 'so called espionage' as a part of greater plan to mislead the Allied Forces. This is one of those examples, where time changes the perception of good and bad works. Probably, all of us know about the role of legendary boxer, Muhammad Ali during Vietnam War!

There is a Russian story (I heard from a very senior officer during an open speech) which goes like this:

One landlord brought one beautiful horse for his young son. On the very first day the son fell down from the horse and broke his leg. Everybody in the village cursed the horse. But on the next day, there was decree from the king that every abled bodied person should join the army and would be sent to the border. Everybody in the village opined that the horse was indeed a lucky one for the young son of the land lord as he need not have to go for the ensuing battle. But after one month, all the villagers had come back from the frontier unscathed as battle did not take place. However, all were given certificates along with monetary benefits from the royalty for their loyalty and bravery. Then, everybody blamed the horse again. And the story goes on.

Therefore, to identify good luck/good work and bad luck/bad work is real tough. So, every day, I question myself, 'Have I done any good work? How many bad works I have done in the last 24 hours? How many hours, I remain idle? Have I done enough work to become a human being?' Normally I do not get an answer which can convince me.

Is it that difficult to become a human being? Perhaps, yes.

When we say a person is mentally ill? If the person is not normal, we call him/her mentally ill or more rudely call him/her 'Mad".

When we call a person normal?

If the behaviour of the person is in conformity with most of the people, we call him/her a normal person.

Up to this point, hopefully everyone will agree with me. As a corollary to this assumption, if any person does not fall within the 3 sigma limit or 5 sigma limit(as you decide) for any attribute associated with 'human being' than he is not a normal person. So if a person fail to perform any of the normal duties of a citizen, son/ daughter, husband/wife, son-in-law/daughter-in-law, father/mother, father-in-law /mother-in-law, brother/ sister, brother-in-law/sister-in-law, senior/junior, boss/ subordinate etc., he/she is not normal as far as that attribute is concerned.

Some of us, we perform our duties of a father/mother better than an average father/mother, but we may fail to perform duties of a son/daughter towards our parents. List is endless. Now, hopefully you understand why I fail to become (normal) human being, despite of my best efforts to become a 'human being'

But my pursuit to become a human being remain as strong as a small kid, I did have.

Chapter: 8

Connecting two rivers

During a dream a few years back, I was travelling through a country side of Assam. The metal road was very straight and it was running side by side of a river. I was surprised to see the straightness of the river. I asked the driver, why the river was so straight. He said that it was not a river but a canal dug by a king of sixteenth century. It connects two major rivulets of Barak River, viz. Gadadhar and Jaymati.

During the rainy season, before the canal was dug, Gadhadhar River used to make havoc and it flowed in such a way that, as if it wanted to meet Jaymati River.

The King Kanhaya Lal thought if with a canal both the rivers would be joined, then his subjects might be saved from the fury of the river, Gadadhar.

As per the plan, he ordered to make a canal connecting the rivers. But just before the completion of the project (only about 20 feet was left for completion of the connecting canal), due to advice of a sadhu, he had to stop the ongoing project.

The sadhu told the King, if he would complete the canal he had to lose his kingdom. Fearing of losing the kingdom, he ordered to stop the work of the canal immediately.

After a week, a few villagers saw some young people led by the crown prince was playing/doing something on the unfinished part of the canal beyond dusk. In the next morning, all the people were surprised to see that both the rivers were connected, but the crown prince and his friends were missing. Even after many days of frantic searches, the king could not find any trace of the crown prince and his friends.

It is believed that the prince with the help of some of his trusted friends completed the canal in that night and in the process he and his friends lost their lives.

As predicted by the sadhu, the King had to lose his kingdom because of an invasion by a neighboring king.

However, due to the canal, fury of flood in the area reduced a lot and therefore even now, the local people worship the prince and his friends as their savior gods.

At this point I woke up. I could not sleep rest of the night. A question haunted me even after many years, again and again, 'Will any of the modern time crown prince/ princesses will sacrifice his /her life for his/ her subjects in such a way?'

Chapter: 9

A letter received from an old friend of mine

I am reproducing a letter from an old friend of mine received few years back.

Dear Hiranya,

After our silver jubilee (anniversary), I slowly start 'dis-loving' (Is there any word like this?) my wife and finally, after five years, I have a feeling that I do not love her anymore! I really feel sorry for her. During the last 30 years, she has given me wonderful company and also gave me two most precious gifts, a wife ever can give to her husband.

During last 30 years, she gained lots of weight and lost lot of attractiveness. Her skin is not so smooth. Her hairs are no more black and silky. Her teeth are also not sparkling white while she smiles. Probably, she also felt same thing about me. Somebody advised me to divorce her? But I could not take his advice for the following reasons:

a) I feel her in my blood as if she is the force which circulates my blood.

b) When I breathe, I feel as if she pumps my heart.

c) When I see something, I feel as if I am looking through her eyes only.

d) When I hear something, I feel it is filtered through her ears only.

e) When she hurts herself (physically, mentally, emotionally), I feel the pain inside my chest.

f) When she smiles, it gives me an eternal happiness.

g) When she does not scold me on trivial issues, I fear if she might be not well.

h) When I am hurt, tears come out from her eyes.

i) When I go out and come late, she scolds me fearing something might have happened to me.

j) When I feel pain, she becomes a worried lady.

k) When she goes to her mother's place she wants to pre-pond her journey back home.

l) After a fight when we do not talk each other for few days, I get my breakfast, lunch and dinner in time. During that period, if somebody (except any of the children) visits us, she behaves normally, as if nothing has happened.

And there are many more similar reasons, why I cannot think of living without her. If you can advise me a way for coming out of the situation, I shall be grateful.

Sincerely yours friend,

Vedanta

I did not write back to him even after many ears on that issue as I have been envious about him.

Chapter: 10

Lesson learnt by Kanak

It is a story about a loser. His name is Kanak (Gold). His parents, both school teachers, gave the name thinking that he would dazzle like gold in his life. But his life turned out differently –like 'dhutura', a fruit from which a kind of drug is extracted for manufacturing country liquor in the country side. He is lanky but he was not in the list of 'dream boy' of any contemporary girls: at least look-wise and smartness-wise.

During his early life, he fought valiantly whenever he had faced any sort of problems created by his own family members and created by someone else. Sometimes, he was able to win and sometimes he lost miserably. But he was a fighter. In school days, he was taunted as a boy from most backward village of the area. He answered it by topping in the class. Parents thought, he was not as smart as his brothers, he proved it otherwise, whenever, he got even ten percent chance.

After, passing out class X examination from the school he joined the most reputed college of the state, where again he had to fight for his existence and to keep his head high. It was not known, whether he was successful or not; but the moot point is that, he had to fight all along, all alone with or without success in his life.

As many of his friends said, he won the election for editor of the college magazine with the support of a particular student organization (not as organizational candidate –as many of his peers thought). Then, what went wrong with organization? He did not have any political ambition like many of the student leaders of that time. When schools and colleges were closed for an indefinite period, he tried to open up a front for opening of schools and holding of examinations etc. That itched the leadership of the organization due to obvious reason. Finally, due to the pressure built up by many of them schools and colleges were reopened. In his edition of the college magazine, he raised some pertinent questions regarding solution of the agitation, international obligations etc. to the then President of the organization. But he did not reply, instead another leader replied, without answering any of his pin pointed questions.

By the time, he was dropped by them (the Student organization and others) like a hot potato. During that period he was approached by some of the leaders from some political parties and tried to persuade him to write articles directly attacking the agitation. Since he did not oblige them, he became a person who is pariah for both the groups. But, once his limited goal of reopening school and colleges was achieved and he came out of that circle.

The economic reason for not writing is also stem out from his economic background. As, already mentioned that, he is a son of a village school teacher parent (Both were teachers). At a particular period of time, all the children of his parents were in hostel. One can understand, what a financial hardship, they might have to undergo. During that period, he used to get a paltry Rs.10/- or Rs.20/- for a published article in a magazine.

Considering the efforts and time spent, it was nothing but peanuts at that time also.

His mother became unhappy with him, as some of his writing created some controversy at social, political and family circles. Reportedly, his sister also had to face some problems in her school due to some of his articles.

By the time he attained the age of 20, he learnt a few lessons of life and realized few things which had changed his course of life.

1. Since he does (did) not have any political ambition, he should not write any politically sensitive article. At one time, he had a limited mission to try to sensitize the people in general, and the students, in particular, to mobilize public opinion to reopen the schools, which he successfully did though he cannot take the credit out of that, as he was not the only one who wrote that types of articles at that time.

2. A group of people will always try to put him in a place, which will be advantageous for them, without any risk for them. For example, the parents of those students who were studying outside the state (at that time), advocated that school/colleges should not be opened till the aim of the agitation is achieved. He observed during that period, some of the highly educated parents advocated that children of ordinary people should be sent to the schools/colleges with vernacular medium; but during the same period, they had sent their children to the English Medium schools. This phenomenon still exist in Assam.

3. At least, at a time, when he did(does) not have sufficient source of income, if he became(becomes) a writer/painter/poet/player then, he would have been

appreciated, but most of his friends would have run away from him, fearing he might ask for any financial help. So he should do something to earn handsomely and only then he should go for writing etc. as a hobby. He should keep the habit of writing as hobby till that time, he could earn a lot of money by writing/painting etc. as a side income.

4. He also found that, many people who advised him to be brave and swim against the current, but when he asked them to support him in action, they avoided him giving some flimsy ground. He remembers vividly, when college hostels were closed by College authority, many local leaders (mostly elderly ladies) asked the hostellers not to vacate whatever might come on the way. But when a question was raised by him, whether all the aunts present at that time, would take at least one hosteller to their homes, for few days, if situation warranted, they refused bluntly and advised, the hostellers to sacrifice even their lives for the country. They showed unhappiness for raising such type of petty (?) questions by Kanak. A few months after, exactly the situation had arisen. The college hostel was raided by CRPF and all the students were taken to the police station. Though they were released afterward, due to fear factors, 99% students had left the hostel except few like him, who did not have any relatives in the city nor had sufficient money to hire a hotel accommodation nor distance between hometown and Guwahati was very less. Then he realized that, first he has to acquire sufficient strength to swim against the current, even if he wants, otherwise, when he is on the mat even his family members, not necessarily by all, may condemn him, forget about others. During the raid also, Kanak showed exemplary bravery by not abandoning the juniors at the

mercy of the CRPF personnel, what many of the seniors actually did. But who cares for that type of bravery?

5. When one has to fight, if no option is left out, one should fight with one at a time. One should not open many fronts at a time. Otherwise, he is bound to be doomed.

6. He observed in his life, everybody wants to advise others to be most idealistic, brave enough to sacrifice everything for the welfare of the state/ society/family etc. However, these types of advices are not given to their loved ones.

Many more lessons he learnt, but only some important lessons are mentioned here.

After realizing those facts of life, Kanak stopped writing any article, short story, novel and poem since 1982 which almost coincided with his joining in Delhi University as a Master Degree student in 1981.

From above, it is clear that, the reasons for not writing anything in the last 31 years are many. But he thinks, the main reason is that, he is not getting proper motivation or any emotional inspiration or any emotional support from the ones who are most important to him. Then, one day, one question struck him, whether, he should pour all his emotion in black and white or not. If yes, then again another question will arise, why now? What inspires him? Or who inspires him?

Whatever may be the reason, he started writing once again from his heart and he earned a name also in the literary world.

Chapter: 11

Sleeping with some unknown persons

Hsssssssssssssssssssssss. Do not tell my wife about this! Before I narrate the story, I just want to know, whether have you ever shared a bed with two to three unknown fellows? I did once in 1989 in a hotel at Calcutta (Kolkata).

Do not worry; it is nothing scandalous.

During that period, I, a young officer of 26, was posted at Kohima as Regional Assistant Director, popularly known as RAD, Nagaland, NSSO (FOD).

I was to take a flight from Guwahati (Guwahati) to Calcutta (Kolkata) to catch a train from Howrah to Hyderabad to attend All India Training Conference for 45th/46th Round of NSSO survey. I came to Guwahati one day before my plan of departure from Guwahati to Kolkata.

My flight was at 8.00 AM from Guwahati to Kolkata. A day before my departure, Indian Airlines announced that my flight would depart at 5 PM only; thanks to 10 hour (From 6 AM to 4PM) Bandh Call given by All

Guwahati Students Union. From here onwards, my ordeal started.

During those years in Assam, a Bandh call given by ASSU/AGSU is like imposition of curfew in a city. Though, many of my friends and family members had cars/scooters, none could muster the courage to drop me at the airport by their cars/scooters. Finally, I decided to stay overnight at the residence with my wife's uncle who lived at University campus. Thus, I reduced the distance to the airport by 8 km.

On the fateful day of departure from Guwahati, I started walking to the airport at around 11AM. It was not a very hot September day of Guwahati therefore I could walk at a brisk speed with my small suitcase. During those days I did not have a trolley bag.

I reached the airport by 2 PM with some helping hands from an airport staff (he gave a lift for 5 km) and an ambulance (I did not fall ill, the driver, on request, gave me a lift for another 2 KM) out of total distance of 18 KM from my relative's residence.

I thought, I would be the only person who braved the Bandh to reach the airport. On reaching the airport, I saw a swarm of passengers who slept on the floor of the airport or elsewhere. No flight from Guwahati was cancelled on that day and all the passengers were accommodated by adjusting flight timing from Guwahati to Delhi and Calcutta. In those days there was no direct flight from Guwahati other than Delhi and Calcutta.

My flight finally departed at 7 PM instead of 5 PM as earlier announced. As flight was late, AI was kind enough to provide coupons for snacks to the passengers. The restaurant was crowded and I managed to get a seat along with three other unknown passengers. As a matter of luck, all four of us, were going to take the same flight for catching trains from Kolkata, precisely from Howrah to different destinations. None of us was travelling by air for comfort or for luxury but for our compulsion only.

Without any hassles, we reached Kolkata and took a taxi to Howrah. We all rented a room and shared a bed for the rest of the night to save some money. In the morning, we all left the hotel, one by one, to go to our different destinations. We have never met again and now, I have already forgotten their names and faces as well.

When, I recall about that day, I feel I did a grave mistake by saving few hundred bucks. Nothing had happened in that night, it is our luck and fortunately, all of us were real and honest passengers. Nowadays, we read many stories, how people are robbed/murdered after befriending with strangers. Whenever, I say about that night, each and every near and dear ones scolds me. Though, I must admit, at the back of the mind, I enjoyed the incident very much.

Chapter: 12

Taste of Food

Have you remember the food which you have cherished most? The best food ever anybody have tasted is his/her mother's milk after his/her birth. Therefore, I am asking about the next best food or tasty food (not necessarily the best food), what you have taken in your life time.

By the grace of God, I have already tasted food from seven star hotels to road side dhaba of most of the capital cities of India. I have also tasted food in many large cities across the world. I have also taken food in many rural areas of the country. Many a times, I had to take food from open food stalls where volume of food increases without any incremental food value as rain fall increases. Sometimes, I have to consume half cooked food and some time, over cooked food. Somctimes, I had consumed good quality food and sometimes I have to consume very bad food. My contention is that, as somebody rightly referred about me that, I am carrying well instead of a stomach and a tongue without any taste bud, I can consume all sorts of food without any complain. Though nowadays, I also restrict my food consumption in terms of quantity due to old age.

So, you may ask me, how I can cherish food without iota of preference for good food as such! But, as you know, sometimes unexpected things happen from an unexpected corner in everyone's life more than once.

Yes, still I remember the date when I took the second best tasty food in my life. It was 5th January, 1980.

I was with a medical team of young group of doctors from Dibrugarh Medical College to visit some injured persons who were allegedly injured in a police firing incident at Duliajan refinery. Along with the doctors, Shri Swapan Sharma, the then Debating Secretary of Cotton College and I were travelling in two Ambassador Cars.

We started our journey at around 8 O'clock in the morning hoping that we shall take our lunch somewhere on the way. Since the injured persons were scattered over a very large area, it took a lot of time to visit each and every one injured in the incident. Most of the persons, whom we had visited, were so poor that they could not offer us anything to eat in the whole day. Further, as we were far away from the main town, we could not find any eateries on the road/villages we had visited.

Our problems enhanced further, when one of the two cars broke down at around six in the evening. The driver tried his best to repair the vehicle, but he could not fix the problem and he had to abandon the idea to repair the vehicle at around 8 PM. So all the occupants of the abandoned car also came to other car, totaling the passenger strength to 12 in the car, excluding the driver. One can easily understand the plight of the passengers in such a situation.

At 11 PM, we reached the highway connecting Naharkatia and Dibrugarh and finally we found a dhaba which was about to be closed at that time. The dhaba owner, told us that there was nothing left substantial to eat. Moreover, he was not in a position to cook anything for us at that hour.

After repeated plea from us, he agreed to give all the stale rootis (Indian bread), which were kept for giving to the stray dogs in the morning and a small bowl of cold dal. But after examining the quantity of available dal, he said that dal might not be enough unless some cold water would be added. Having no alternative, dal was mixed with cold water and served to us alongwith two state roties to each one of us.

Please imagine, in an ordinary condition, in the month of January, stale rootis with cold watered dal, if it is served to someone what will be his/her reaction! But believe me, all of us took the served food with all excitement and licked the utensils where dal was served. We found the taste of the rooties and dal was extremely good and all of us praised the cook of the hotel for his magnificent skill of cooking. In my opinion, that was the second best food I have ever taken in my six decades of colourful life.

Chapter: 13

Success story of a Fighter

Deepak, a close friend of Kanak is a winner all the way in his life due to his fighting spirit.

Why he is successful in quelling all the disadvantages on the way for his progress? In most of the cases, he made the hurdles of his life as the stepping stones of his progress. I shall narrate one of those stories which he confided with me few years back.

Deepak is from a rural humble background. Though, he was brilliant in his studies, due to economic background, he used to think that after matriculation, even if he would get a post of a peon in a Government office, he would have been satisfied. After passing out from the school, he joined the same reputed college where I also studied. He was allotted the adjacent hostel where I used to stay.

The incident what Deepak had narrated to me, could have devastated very life of Deepak, but Deepak not only withstood it but made a turning point out for him, for the betterment of his career.

It was 9 O'clock in the evening, after a stroll, Deepak observed that, in the corridor, a heated argument was going on amongst some of the boarders of the hostel.

After some time, a meeting was called to discuss an important issue (sic!) among the hostellers. Till then, Deepak was not aware, what was the subject matter of the meeting. Once he reached the meeting, he was told that because of him and one of his friends, the some of the hostellers (they were from upper/upper middle class families and were also most vocal and dominating in the hostel) were embarrassed due to some of their actions. He was perplexed, he thought, according to him, he had done nothing wrong.

'What is our fault?' Deepak asked.

Then he was told that his friend and he used to stroll outside hostel wearing lungi and vests which, according to them, lowered the prestige of the other hostellers. Then, his friend and he were warned that if they would continue to do so they would be thrown out of the hostel.

He did not utter a single word because he knew that at that time he was not in a position to fight back. Neither, he had another pair of shirt and trouser to go out of hostel after dinner.

After that day onwards, he stayed back in his room after dinner and concentrated in his studies. Today, he thanked all those rogues for their actions as he feels because of their actions he studied more and he could manage to have better results in his studies than those students.

Now, he is holding a very senior and influential post in Government but keeps his feet on firm ground of honesty and allegiance to his duties. I salute him for his fighting spirit and consider him as a winner all the way.

PS: There is nothing wrong of being a son/daughter of rich/influential persons. But if you are a son/daughter of rich person, then your heart also should be large enough to accommodate honesty, empathy for the poor and so on. The boarders of the hostel, who were from upper/upper middle class could have presented him two pairs of dresses on his birth day with a caveat that he should go out for the evening stroll with proper dress code. Then perhaps, he would have thought about them differently. I do not know about all of them, what position they are holding today. But I am damn sure none of them is holding any better post than Deepak. It is not only in India, but also anywhere in the world in general, and in the third world, in particular, we are more proud of our linage than what we are. Even President Abraham Lincoln was once taunted by his adversaries for his linage. But Lincoln shot back that, he was proud of his parents and forefathers not for the job they were doing but for their honesty and their sincerity in performing their duties/jobs. I may be holding a better post than Mr. X, but if he is performing his duties more sincerely and honestly, then his children should be more proud of him, than my children for me. But unfortunately, normally we do not do that.

Chapter: 14

Whom I love most? Is it time specific?

What I am going to write here, you may agree, you may disagree, you may condemn it, but before doing that, just ask the questions to yourself, I have posed for you, 'Whom do you love most?' Is it yourself or someone else?

A friend of mine told about himself like this: 'As a normal child, I used to love my mother most, till the age of 12. Then, I met a girl, I thought, I love her most. At that time, my world starts with her and ends with her. During that period, lasting for five to six years, I did not even think of living without her. Now, she does not appear in my list of persons whom I love.' Does it mean that, love is a time specific state of mind only?

I do not want to tell my personal encounters with love before my marriage. So, as a family man, in this article, I start my odyssey of love after my marriage.

After I got married and as a 'Jaru ka gulam' (wife's obedient servant), I was officially in love with her till my daughter was born. This is the turning point of my love affairs after my marriage. In due course of time, I have been blessed with my son and my younger daughter. Now, there are four main contenders (after expiry of my mother), at least officially, for the top 'my most loved one' list.

The first contender is my wife-being the only one in that category, she thinks that it is her legitimate right to walk away with the 'most loved one' trophy from me.

My elder daughter claims her stake, being the eldest child of the family.

My son's claim also have lot of credentials being the only son of our family.

Do not underestimate the weakest / most diminutive person of the family, my youngest daughter, for the title. She is the most adorable and pampered child of the family.

But whom do I love most?

Some time, my wife withdraws from the race. But other three will not budge a single inch from their claims. As a diplomatic person, I have not shown any inclination to any of the three contenders for the top status. However, over the years, I realized that love for mother/father and vice versa, never diminish, but flows like a strong undercurrent in large rivers like Brahmaputra, Amazon etc. Love for others is fluctuating like waves of a sea.

Love has also many components like any other earthly materials. Considering one criteria, I may grade three of them (my children) in a sequence. Again for another criteria, I can rank them differently. After giving ranking for all the criterion, I shall attach weight on different criteria. As a true statistician, I can find out an index and rank them in my list of the most loved one.

But there is another problem. As a normal person, my mood also swings. Therefore, I have to have a time series data, instead of a one set of data which may lead to an erroneous result. So, I am facing lot of problems in finding a solution at my level. Is anybody facing similar type of problems so far? Those having single child, the problem is easier to solve, till the second one arrives.

The problem, I faced may be a modern one. Earlier, even a father might have a dozen children, but all the children were aware that whom the father loved most/least etc. Even my father did not have any such type of problems in his decision making process. All the children, he had, knew whom he loved most and whom he loved least. Once my wife overheard, when my father was saying to my son (at that time he was the only male grandson of our family and he was only seven year old) that, he is the most loved one for him. Even all the other grandchildren constitute only 40% of his love space in his heart. You can understand, how uncanny he was!

Arrival of new one into a family always, alters the love equation in any normal family. The new member of the family may be eagerly awaited one, may be the most un-expected one, may be the desired one, may be the undesirable one, contender for most loved one, contender for the most hated one, periphery-able, centric one and so on. Some time, it creates lot of ripples, sometime it comes without any ripple. Some time, new one settles for anything and another one wants everything. But problem remains. Is the equation in the family is heavily dependent on 'time'. Take the example of arrival of a new daughter in law in a family. She is adored for some time. Then----.

Like security cordon of PM, there are so many layers, not necessarily competing each other, of persons whom you love and who may also love you. To illustrate the system of love, let me remind you (I am sure, all of you know this system), that the inner circle is occupied by your children, wife and parents (unmarried siblings are also included some times), second layers consist of cousins, close friends, other close relatives and third layer consists of rest of the cousins, friends, relatives and others. Intentionally, I have left out the in laws. They are in the extreme categories: either in the second category of loved ones or they are in the most hated categories.

At the end of the 'love circle', the circle of 'like circle' starts. Difference between love and like is very blurred. At any point of time, 'liked' people can enter to 'loved' people category and vice versa. Sometimes, it does not create problem, sometime it may invite storm. The particles (persons) in the 'love circle/like circles' are floating and moving around you, changing their routes, sometimes marginally and sometimes very significantly.

Another very interesting circle is the 'Fan (club) circle'. It is very interesting to note that, some fans are so obsessed with their idols that, they may go up to any extent. There are some examples of extreme cases, where some fans commit suicide after hearing the news of death of one of their idols. The opposite example of such cases is, killing of John Lennon by a fanatic fan.

There is another circle, where people stand for a minute/ hour/day/ week depending upon different situation, when we think the friendship/relationship will last long, but unfortunately, it evaporates quicker than camphor. Best example of this type of relation (love affair), is meeting people in a conference/ travel etc. There is another overlapping circle, love with respect. This circle is probably, the most divine one, where a very few number of people reside and there are very few changes possible in your life time.

As I am trying to explain the love affairs digitally, let me try to explain the coordinates of system as well. We can associate each criteria as one coordinate and it becomes a multivariate exercise.

Who are the major players? I put 'time' as the most dominating factor. Sometimes, money may also play an important role. Feeling of security is another factor. Sometimes, it may not be common, but very strong factor is 'Blind love'. It is really difficult to decipher that factor. I am giving an interesting narration what my maternal uncle had told me few years back.

Once he was approached by a father of one of the students whom he had taught in school, to persuade his son to abandon the idea to marry a very ugly divorcee, older than his son. But when my uncle tried to rack up the issue, he interrupted, 'Sir, I know what you want to say! But please see through my eyes, you will see her as the most beautiful lady you have ever seen!' My uncle did not utter a single word and left the boy for living with his own destiny.

Can you solve my problem? Or I am confusing you further? If you have more than one child, you must have encountered, at least once, this particular question from the younger one, 'Do you love me most?'

Most interesting part of the system is that, nobody fights over 'who loves you most?' Not necessarily, the person whom you love most, also loves you most. In some extreme cases, the person whom you love most, actually hates you! Normally, we expect reciprocal feelings- but how many of us are lucky enough to get reciprocal love with equal intensity?

Chapter: 15

Good person v/s bad person

We casually comment about a person as good or bad. But the moot question is, who is good and who is bad.

Take for example; a person is regarded as a very good person, by majority of your acquaintances. But he has hurt your interest/sentiment; will you still regard him/her as a good person?

Again a person is known for his notoriety, but he helped once your child/wife when they were in distress and no one, so called, any of the good persons, came forward to help your child/ wife. Will you still call him/her a bad person?

In my opinion there is no good person or bad person- only there may be a good work and bad work.

We call a person good or bad depending upon his actions towards you, not necessarily to all the persons around him/her. If his/ her actions anyway affect your interest/sentiment, he is not a good person for you otherwise he is a good person, till he /she hurts you.

In other words, good person or bad person is not an 'absolute' but a 'perceptional' quality.

Chapter: 16

Good work v/s Bad work

Then, what is a good work or a bad work?

Yes, there are some good works where majority of the people are benefitted and there are some bad works when majority of the people are adversely effected.

Again the question arises, whether will of the minority (I am not referring constitutional minority etc.) should be ignored, even though their will may be more justified than the will of the majority.

For any activity, we say good or bad, depending upon on which side of the conflict you are standing. In an extreme example, all the rebels are either treated as hero or villain depending upon to whom you are lending your moral/ financial/ physical/ all out support.

At micro level, one action of yours may be appreciated by one neighbour/ relative/friend as a good work, the other neighbour/ relative/ friend may condemn the same action as a very bad work.

However, there may be some actions of yours may be either appreciated/condemned by one and all. For example, donating of blood, helping the marooned persons, helping the poor etc. are regarded as good work universally- but unfortunately, we seldom do it.

I know many parents, who agree that blood donation is a noble work, but always advise their children not to donate blood. Does it mean that all bookish good works, are not to be followed in letter and spirit?

There were some persons including some of my close friends, who became very emotional on seeing how military persons are helping the marooned persons in Uttarakhand few years ago when more than thousand perished and more than lakh people became homeless due to unprecedented flood. They forward some very emotional messages to all the persons known to them with a request to forward the message with another sentimental dialogue 'if you agree' with the underlying message that we should send our children to join armed forces not to become civil servants, engineers and so on.

But I am hundred percent sure that most of them will not send their children to the military nor send their wards to the site of the disaster to help the marooned persons.

I do not know, whether sending/forwarding such type of messages are good work or not, but I am sure, that will not help the marooned people.

Therefore, in my opinion, one should do that work, which is driven by his/ her own conscience, not by public opinions and there is some positive impact on the ground. Even you need not have to agree with my opinion!

This article is dedicated to all the blood donors, military and volunteers who lost their lives while rescuing marooned people.

Chapter: 17

Those 54 days of my life

Life has some defining moments. For example, for Usain Bolt, those 9.58 seconds are the defining moments for him and for the world as a whole, when he created world and Olympic record in 100 metre sprint.

But for me 'those 54 days' are the most defining days of my life when my wife was hospitalized in Guwahati Medical College GMC). Out of 54 days of hospitalization, she was in coma for 22 days and another 15 days she was in a semi-coma stage.

Before unfolding the pain and ecstasy of those days, let me thank all the persons who helped me during that period in different ways. Special mention I would like to make, other than my family members and family members of my in laws, Prof. Ajaya Mahanta and her team of doctors and nurses of GMC, Late Shri S. N. Bhuyan, the then Regional Director, Staff Selection Commission(SSC), Shri B. Dey, the then Assistant Director, SSC, Shri Touthang, the then Assistant Director, SSC, Shri Ghanashyam, the then Regional Assistant Director, NSSO(FOD) and his team (Particularly, Govinda, Tushar, Hemanga and S.K. Das), Shri Chandrajit Saikia, IRPS, Prof. S. Choudhury Sir & Sovita Baideu, my neighbours, Shri Naresh Kumar

Sharma, ISS and host of visitors who gave me all sorts of supports. If I forget to mention any name here, I apologize for that. However, I deliberately do not want to mention any name of my own and my wife's relatives.

From 3rd October, 1995, my wife had been complaining about an awkward pain on her right calf muscle. By 5th October, she lost control over call of nature and immediately she was hospitalized after a brief consultation with Dr. Bipul Barua, our family doctor and my father in law who was a Retired Head of the Department of Pharmacology of Assam Medical College and Guwahati Medical College.

Prof. Ajaya Mahanta, the then Head of Neurology, GMC, a meritorious student of my father in law, advised us to take her for a CT scan. As per advice I took her to the CT scan laboratory and had done the CT scan. However, nothing could be diagnosed in the CT scan report. Unfortunately, from that midnight, she had gone into the state of coma. She was administered Decadron injection but without any success.

After two days, after doing MRI scanning, she was diagnosed as she had been under viral attack on her brain myelin (cover of brain) (shortly diagnosed as Encephalomyelitis) and administered Methylprednisolone (a synthetic glucocorticoid or corticosteroid drug. It is used to treat conditions such as allergies, arthritis, lupus and ulcerative colitis with lot of side effects, interactions and indications.).

The medicine (injection) was very costly (at that time it was Rs.840/- per injection, my salary was about Rs.7200/- pm as Deputy Director, SSC, Government of India). They recommended eight injections for eight days (one injection per day). The injection was so strong that it could be injected through saline only and should take 20-30 minutes for injecting one dose. Further, to avoid any ill effects of the medicine, seventeen different types of medicines were to be given three times daily for next eight days.

Canola was inserted on her wrist for continuous feeding of saline (sodium nitrates/ phosphate etc). Cotton was placed on her eyes and eye drops were given so that her eyes were not damaged. Liquid food along with all oral medicines was given through a nose pipe and a catheter was used for urination.

After 10 days of her coma, I started thinking that she would survive and asked to Prof. Koyal, who was also attending my wife from the very beginning, 'What is the chance of her survival now?'

He told me candidly, 'Yes her chance of survival has increased now, from zero to 1% as her condition has not further deteriorated.'

I was speechless for some time.

On 15th day, I was called by Prof. Mahanta to her chamber and told categorically that, there was very little chance that she would survive. She also informed that, she had been disturbed by the behaviour of some of my wife's relatives. However, she also said that, she had no intention to blame them, as it is very common, when patient does not improve, the doctors are blamed for inefficiency or negligence on their part. But, as legal guardian of the patient, I should have the last call. She asked me whether, I wanted to shift her to some other hospital within Guwahati or to shift to Delhi as advised by some of the relatives of my wife.

Then, I recalled that, some of the visitors/distant relatives of my wife, had made remarks before some of the junior doctors accusing inefficient handling / negligence on the part of doctors. I also could remember, some of my wife's relatives had advised me to take my wife to Delhi by air by booking four to five seats as she would be in lying posture only.

I told Dr. Mahanta that, I had full faith in God and her and I was sure that she (my wife) would be alright after few days.

Dr. Mahanta assured me of her full attention to my wife but she also told me that there is only a very slim chance of her recovery. Further, she told me that even if she survives, she might be paralytic and might have to be on her bed for the rest of her life.

I told her, 'Do whatever is possible and rest is only God's hand. I assure you madam, if anything goes wrong; I shall be the last man to blame you.'

When I discussed this with my father and father in law, they also lost hope for my wife. They gradually prepared mentally for any eventuality and they also discussed about my children's future in case, my wife would be paralytic or would die. What they had decided, I do not want to discuss here, as both of them are no more today; but I did not agree to their proposal.

On the seventeenth day, I asked my sister in law to bring my children to the hospital to see their mother for the last time, might be. When they came to meet her, that was the first and last time, I lost my composure for a while and I could not stop my tears-otherwise I was so busy in attending her, I could not show any emotion, whatsoever, for those 54 days.

My daughter, who was 9 and son, 7 years, sat at the bedside their mother for some time, with moist eyes. My daughter murmured, 'Ma, if you die, with whom I shall argue on trivial issues.'

My son did not utter a single word throughout his stay with his mother.

On the 23rd day, she murmured something when I was alone. I told the visiting doctor about it, but he did not believe it. On the next day she said something which was also not properly audible and again I told the doctor about her utterances. The doctor smiled; but did not say anything.

From 25th day, she started to scream and told me something irrelevant whenever I was alone with her. When I reported to Dr. Mahanta, she referred me to a psychologist, whose wife happened to be a classmate of mine.

Initially, I thought I was sent to him to discuss about my wife's impending psychological problem, but subsequently I realized that he was testing my mental condition only.

All doctors whom I talked about uttering words by my wife, were in the opinion that I was so exhausted in attending my wife, I lost my mental balance(influence of hallucination).

When on the next day, my wife uttered something, I told my wife, 'Why you do not utter any word when someone else is also present? Doctors are thinking that I am going to be a mad man soon.'

With a clear voice she told me, 'I rely on you only.' Then she again closed her eyes.

I was in a great dilemma, whether I should tell others about her coming to sense or not. Luckily for me, on that evening, she uttered a single word in presence of my brother in law.

I requested my brother in law to write a line or two for the doctors so that I should not be thought of losing mental balance.

For the next two days, she spoke many words; most of them did not carry any meaning. Finally, on the 37th day, she started talking meaningfully when my cousin told her that, how much pain I was taking for her. She politely requested him to take care of me.

Her cotton covers were removed from her eyes and by the 40th day, nasal food pipe was also removed and food was administered through mouth.

By the 45th day, she started sitting on the bed with some assistance from the attendant. In between, catheter and canola were also removed and she was finally wheeled to my in laws residence on the 55th day.

I stayed with her 54 days and 49 nights (four nights when I was not with her, shared by my brother in law, one neighbor and one of my cousins).

She took another one month or so, to walk normally after release from her hospital and had to take medicines for another six months.

After, two years, she was again hospitalized for giving birth of our little angel on 07.05.1998.

What I learnt from those 54 days, let me share with you:

1. Always believe in God, attending doctors and yourself.

2. Take all the responsibilities with full of conviction.

3. Do as much as possible for the patient, stretch it to the maximum and if possible, do other's duties also. I seldom called the nurses to give medicines, change saline, slept minimum to attend her for maximum time. I never called ward boy/dhai to administer enema for her bowl or changing clothes or changing bed sheets or messaging the body (physiotherapist taught me how to do it) or changing the toilet bowl. These may be very small things, but these give confidence to the patient.

4. Do not be emotional and try to maintain your composure as much as possible. I also lost temper many a times, when some of my/ my in laws relatives tried to advise me, how to attend patient, who never attended any patient in their whole life. But, afterwards, I realized, I should not have reacted the way I did; because, after all, they are also passive well-wishers of my wife, even if they might not be well-wishers of mine.

5. I understood, 50% visitors are coming to meet me and express their solidarity with me genuinely, and rest are coming either to fulfill social obligation or to shed crocodile's tear. Some are coming only for a much needed outing to pass their time outside home.

6. Doctors/Physiotherapists have common presumptions that husbands are not taking care of their wives when they are down with some or other types of ailments. Their presumptions are also coming out from their experiences. During my stay in the hospitals, I saw many husbands are not willing to touch the cloths of their ailing wives, forget about nursing. Many husbands are

relishing chicken/ mutton when their wives are in operation theatre. Once I overheard one father asked his teen aged son to accompany him to the restaurant when his wife was inside the operation theatre, 'Let us go to restaurant to take something as we have no work for the next 3-4 hours.' When the son refused to go, he scolded his son, 'Are you a doctor? Only doctor will operate, not you?' I understand his argument. But I have seen when husbands are in an operation theatre, except for few exceptions; no wife is willing to leave the benches kept outside the operation theatre.

7. In the lighter side, though 100% true, I want to share something about feeling of some visitors. One visitor was saying, if my wife became paralytic, I should not marry, because there would be lot of quarrel between the two wives. One visitor advised me to search for suitable match once all rituals are over (he was 100% sure that my wife would not survive). Another visitor advised me to marry any of my unmarried sister in law (he was also 100% sure my wife would not survive), as only a sister- in law, as stepmother might love my orphaned children. Nowadays, to tease my wife, I tell her how she had spoiled my chance to have a new wife, by surviving a life threatening ailment.

8. And finally, I realized (sic), every relative of my wife cares my wife more than me through their over-zealous concerns.

This article is dedicated to Almighty and team of medicos of GMC led by Prof. Ajaya Mahanta.

Chapter: 18

Etiquette Learnt from a Lecturer

The incident happened in 2002. There was an interactive workshop between NSSO (FOD) officers and Industrial representatives at Tezpur which is about 180 KM from my place of posting, Guwahati.

On that particular day, the Private Bus Association called for a 12 hour Chakka jam (a strike: Assam is infamous for strikes/ Bandh even today). I alongwith an ISS probationer, who was undergoing training at Regional Office, Guwahati, had to attend the workshop at 10 O' clock in the morning.

As usual, I took my Maruti-800 car and picked up the probationer from Ganeshguri Chariali (on the way to Tezpur). At Nagaon (126 KM from Guwahati), after taking our breakfast, when I was about to start my vehicle, a gentle man, in his early 30s approached me with a request to give him a lift to Tezpur, introducing himself as a lecturer in Agriculture University, Tezpur. Considering the fact that, on that day, there was really an acute problem of getting a transport, I obliged without showing any displeasure on my face.

Being a talkative person, I talked with the lecturer and the probationer all the way to Tezpur while driving.

The newly introduced lecturer, he had addressed me as 'sir' every time in our conversations during almost entire journey time.

The lecturer had to get down at Panchmile (Five Miles from Tezpur), just before the entry point of the town. After getting down from the car, he thanked me like this, 'Thank you dada, I shall meet you some time again.'

I was really amused by his address. As he came down from the car, so did he come down from 'sir to dada'. But I did not say anything, as I always think that lecturers are always one up than the Officers in Government in respect of behaviour etc.

This article is dedicated to that particular lecturer, who had taught me how to kick the boat as soon as you get down from it.

Chapter: 19

That 100 metre Distance

The memory of that fateful day (31st October, 1997) is still vivid in my mind.

On that year, Kali Puja and Diwali were observed on 30th October. During that period, I was posted at the Regional Staff Selection Office (North East), Government of India, Guwahati.

On 31st October, except me, only two other officials were present in the office. At around 2-30 PM, I told my Assistant, Mr. Ahmed, that I was also going to leave the office by 3 PM. At that time itself my telephone rang. It was a phone call from my closest friend, Tora from my village.

He told me that my father suddenly had fallen sick so I should come home alongwith my mother and elder brother. When I asked him, what exactly happened to my father, he did not elaborate. But, from the voice of my friend, I was almost sure that my father was no more by that time.

Actually, on that morning itself my mother left home for Shillong, where my sister used to live with her family during those days. Luckily she (my mother) stayed back at by my brother's place on her way to Shillong. During lunch time, I met her at my brother's residence and talked more than one hour with free flowing laughter.

In those days, I did not have a landline phone (need not have to say that there was no mobile phone for the common people at that time in India), though I deposited advance money for it, a few years back. Therefore, had I left my office little bit earlier, my friend would not be able to contact me.

I went to my brother's place immediately by my scooter. My mother was surprised to see me once again within a gap of one hour.

I told my mother to be ready for returning home by the earliest available bus as my father was reportedly fall sick.

She was more surprised to hear the news, as she left my father in the morning in a healthy condition. In fact, my father saw her off at the bus stand which is about 1.5 KM from our home.

At that time, my brother was also not at his home. So, I have to drive my scooter to his office to tell the news.

He consoled me that, since Tora (my friend) telephoned me at my office, our father's condition might not be that bad. Otherwise, how Tora would have known my office number? But, I was adamant that, he should also accompany us to our paternal home without any delay.

On the next day, my niece had an admission test in a reputed school, therefore, my sister in law also insisted that my brother should stay back. But again I insisted, that my brother should come with me. Somehow, I was able to convince them to change their stance.

At 6-30 PM, we took a bus which would go to North Lakhimpur (a district HQs 400 KM away from Guwahati) via my village, Sootea.

By 11-30 PM the bus dropped us at the highway from where our home was about 100 metres away. During the whole journey period, we seldom uttered any word except my mother was repeating the same sentence, 'When I left home, he was perfectly alright. How he can be seriously ill?'

After getting down from the bus, I told my brother to come slowly with our mother as I wanted to go fast. I sped up to cover that 100 metre as fast as possible. But, I thought that 100 metre would not end. It appeared, I was walking for decades to reach my home and finally when I reached home, I was told that my father had expired at 2-15 PM due to massive heart attack.

This article is dedicated to my late father.

Chapter: 20

Respect your needs

A beautiful lady of forty plus, mother of two talented boys aged 16 and 12, an ideal English teacher of a Government School, with a doting husband and cooperative in laws, Anamika tried to commit suicide by poisoning herself. Fortunately, she was saved by a team of dedicated doctors and medicos- of course, due to timely hospitalization by her family members. Everybody, who knows her for years, was surprised by her action.

According to her husband, she was a dream wife, any husband wishes for. According to her students, she was like an elder sister to them, and for seniors, one of the most disciplined and reliable teacher. For her children, she was everything and for her in laws, she was like their own daughter. Then what happened so drastic, that prompted her to take such an extreme step?

Immediately, steps were taken to inform everybody known to her that, she had actually accidently taken poison thinking something else. Every family member was engaged for damage control.

But, what had happened in reality?

Actually, she became fed up with playing the role of an ideal wife, an ideal mother, an ideal daughter in law, an ideal teacher and an ideal human being. She respected every ones sentiment but in the process she stopped thinking that, she was also a normal woman, yes normal woman who needs both physical and mental space, both physical and mental attention from her husband etc. Everybody had taken her for granted. She had been put at pedestal of a demi goddess who could do only good things for someone who is related or known to her, nothing else.

She had never been seen as a woman, but as a mother, a daughter, a wife, a teacher and so on, nobody tried to realize that, she was also a woman of flesh and blood. She seldom got time to talk to her husband on films or any other subjects- which were not related to welfare of children or welfare of the in laws. In school, no joke was shared with her as she was thought to be a serious lady. She was associated with prayers and 'satsang'/ havan etc. only and advices were solicited from her for match making, solving household problems by junior teachers and senior teachers alike. By the time, even love making with her husband had also become a serious matter as she became a respectable mother of two!

She stopped respecting her needs of her body and mind. She stopped caring her beautiful curves on her body, which her husband had also stopped appreciating long back.

A young teacher Rahul joined the school as a French teacher where Anamika was an English teacher. The young boy of twenty-four has a magnetic power to attract anyone who talks with him for few minutes. At first, Anamika wanted to avoid him for his un-necessary talks. But he was different from ordinary talkative person. He noticed that the middle-aged lady teacher was avoiding him. One day, he confronted Anamika.

'Madam, whatever may be the reason, you are trying to avoid me. May I know the reason?'

'To be frank, I do not talk un-necessarily and I do not like to talk to anyone who talks un-necessarily.' Anamika told Rahul candidly.

'I know. But in my opinion, there is nothing un-necessary talks as such. Every, apparently un-necessarily talks actually energize any person to do necessary works in life. But do not worry, I shall not talk to you in future, if you think I talk un-necessarily.' Rahul said with a smile. Then he left her to herself.

Anamika felt bad about her own behavior. She realized that she hurt the young man. She wanted to mend her ways.

When she met Rahul on the next day, she wanted to talk to him. But Rahul did not show any interest in speaking to her. She felt insulted. She told herself, she would never talk to him.

Anamika noticed, Rahul became friendly to everyone except her. She felt alienated and humiliated. After a week, the Principal called Anamika and Rahul to assign a work. They were asked to accompany the selected students for a tournament to be held within the city from the next day. Coming out from the Principal's room, Rahul told Anamika, 'It will be difficult for me to control the students as none is serious about me. I am happy that you will be with me. Everyone in the school is fearful about you!'

Anamika could not understand whether Rahul was praising her or taunting her by saying 'fearful person.' She did not react immediately.

To her surprise, while boarding to the school bus, all the students greeted Rahul with a smile and she was greeted with serious faces. All the students were friendly to him; but they follow his instructions meticulously.

'Madam, I know what you are thinking right now! But time is yet to be over for you! You may also have a second innings!" He smiled meaningfully.

Anamika could not understand what he actually had meant by second innings. She innocently asked, 'What do you mean by a second innings?'

'Madam, you are still very beautiful. You can still compete with young girls like Namrata (a young teacher of her school).' Without removing his eyes from her eyes, he said.

Anamika blushed for the first time, after many years. She could not find an answer to his flirt. On seeing her mum, Rahul said again, 'I am not joking. You are really very beautiful. That is why I was avoiding you. I am preventing myself from falling in love with you.' He smiled again.

Anamika thought to rebuke the young man. But she could not do so. She started liking his flirting. She realized, flirting might also be so beautiful from the young man.

She also started flirting with the young man which she had abandoned long time ago. After one month Anamika realized that she had also fallen in love with the young man. Now without talking to him, she cannot pass her time. Even when she was in the midst of her family, Rahul's face and talks started disturbing her.

Initially, she was not sure, whether Rahul was also in love with her or not. She did not dare to ask Rahul whether he had also same feeling as she had for him. She feared, a rejection from Rahul might demolish her heart.

Rahul was smarter and courageous than Anamika. One day after school he asked Anamika, 'Madam, I decided to call you as Anamika. After all, I cannot call my girlfriend as Madam.'

He did not ask any permission from Anamika to address her by name, but informed his decision. Anamika was surprised to see his audacity. But she liked his approach.

From that day, onwards, he called Anamika by name outside school. One day he invited her for a cup of tea to a restaurant. While in the restaurant, initially he started touching her hands and then her sleeveless arms. She thought to oppose his advances, but she failed to do so due to some unknown reasons. Rather she liked his touches.

Embolden by her silence, one day he invited her for a walk to a nearby park. As they were walking in the park, taking advantage of absence of any person nearby them, he embraced her and smacked few kisses on her cheeks. Again, she could not resist his advances.

But one day when strolling in the park, he kissed her on her lips, she realized he had gone too far.

'I am a teacher and you are also a teacher. We should not cross our limits. Further, I am a wife of a senior officer and mother of two.' She admonished Rahul.

'Now, you are saying that we should stop here after coming so far. I cannot return back from here. I want you. I want to marry you.' He said.

'I cannot leave my family.' Anamika told him sternly. She did not wait for his answer and left the park.

On the next day when she met Rahul, she avoided him. He tried to talk to her. The stalemate continued for one month. The other teachers also observed this. One day, Anamika was told by another teacher that Rahul had resigned from the school to join another job.

Anamika returned back to her boring life once again. She felt nobody had cared for her likings or disliking other than Rahul, whom she had dumped for the very family who never cared for her. She thought deeply about herself, 'I have to think for everyone; but none thinks about me!' This negative thought took over her mind and soul slowly but steadily.

Her unhappiness towards her life continued to grow day by day.

Finally, one day she took that drastic step!

I cannot authenticate veracity of the story, as it was told in a cocktail party few years ago, with lot of salt and spices by a friend. I also cannot say what is right or what is wrong, but in my opinion, one should keep something (may be anything) exclusively for oneself. One should keep some space where nobody except himself/ herself should be allowed to venture and respect himself/herself also along with others before suffocation becomes intolerable.

Chapter: 21

Bitter pill for simplicity

Few years back, when I stopped my car at a red light, a street vendor approached me, 'Babujee kitab le lo. Hindi me barhia novel hei.'

When I refused, he went to another car and requested the passenger, 'Very good novel sir! Take one.'

I realized what prompted his approach to different persons differently. I was driving my old Maruti 800 car and the other person he had approached was the only passenger sitting on the back seat of a Honda City driven a chauffeur.

In those days, as I was holding senior post in Government of India, my children and some of my junior officers (who love me) have been pressing for a new car. However, due to some reasons, which were appreciated by some, I was not in a position to immediately go for a new car- which is definitely not for my simplicity (sic!)

However, here I want to narrate a story about a person who happened to be my senior and had retired few years back.

Once, few years back, I had to travel with him to a nearby city on an official visit, precisely to attend a meeting where many of our service officers had to attend.

Since it was a nearby city, he told me to come along with him by train even though there was air connectivity. Most of the junior officers, particularly those who became eligible to take flights for the first time availed air journey to the city.

On reaching the railway station, we searched for the vehicle which the organizer had promised to send. After frantic search for half an hour for the vehicle (the phone number of the contact person given to us, found to be a wrong number), I contacted one of our own officers. Then, he contacted the organizer to send a vehicle. The concerned officer of the host office initially refused to send a vehicle as according to him, vehicle was supposed to be sent to senior officers only and precisely, those coming by air- not by train.

The officer from our service, told the host officer that, the officer who had been waiting for the vehicle happened to be the senior most officer attending the meeting.

There are many stories about this gentleman for his simplicity-like once he was thought by a probationer as a 'promotee officer' (of his own rank) till, DG introduced him that he was the 2nd/3rd ranked officer of the service.

But, last time when I met him in a social gathering after his retirement, his answer to a simple specific question by an attendant floored me. While offering a cup of tea he was asked by the attendant, 'Sir, would you like to take some sugar?'

'Give me two cubes (sugar).'

Turning to me he said, 'I am not suffering from Diabetes so far. As you have been knowing me for so many years, perhaps you are aware that I had to swallow so many bitter pills for my simplicity.' He smiled quietly.

His answer posed me a lot of un-answered questions only. Is he blessed with healthy body and mind for his simplicity? Is he repenting for his simplicity? Though he never showed any discomfort overtly, when he was ignored, was he actually feeling bad about those incidents? Was he comfortable from within, for his simplicity? Was he simple because of some unknown compulsions rather than by choice?

The article is dedicated to those persons who live like paupers but think like kings.

Chapter: 22

Accidents by school buses/vans

Whenever, there is an accident involving a school bus, from media to common people everybody blames the driver of the bus and the school management.

In the process of criticizing the drivers, we forget to identify the equally responsible culprits for all these accidents.

Wait- do not see me red for the accusation, I am going to make. It is the 'late latif' parents, who are equally, if not more, responsible for reckless driving by the bus/van driver ferrying the innocent children.

I saw the phenomenon of sending their wards at the nick of the time/ late to the bus stands at Guwahati when my two elder children used to take bus ride from Silpukhuri bus stand to the school at Khanapara. Being Assam is known as a land of 'Lahe-lahe'(go slow), I thought it is our birth right to send our wards late to the bus stand and keep the bus waiting for more than the allotted time. Sometimes, parents signaled the bus driver, even after he (the driver) had started, to stop the bus, so that, their towing wards could get into the bus. But after arriving in Delhi, I realized that, this great culture of 'lahe lahe' has not been patented by the people of Guwahati or as a whole the people of Assamese only. In the last few years, I have observed, all the van/bus drivers have been facing this chronic problem from most of the parents of the children.

Please see the plight of the poor driver. He has been given timing for each stoppage. If your ward is late, you will scold him, 'Can't you wait for a minute?'

If he uttered a single word, you will say, 'Do you know, who I am? I shall lodge a complaint against your behaviour to your management.'

In the next stop, another gentleman/lady will scold him for arriving one minute late and with same type of threatening.

So what the poor driver will do! He will press the accelerator more than necessary and jumps the red light quite often. And sometimes, unfortunately, an untoward incident happens.

As, we all know, when our school bus will come, then why can't we manage time accordingly? Time management is a very important aspect in our life. Many brilliant children could not do well in their examinations, because of faulty time management. A child learns many things from his/her parent. Therefore, it is our bounden duty to teach our children about time management along with other important things in our life. Napoleon, the Great, lost in Waterloo only because of his decision to delay the deployment of his Elite force into the combat arena. Some writers even say that, Napoleon lost Waterloo because of only five minutes; though I disagree that statement outright.

I am doubtful that, those parents who cannot send their children to the bus stand in time/ before time, have ever attended office in time. Am I hitting some of our esteemed fellow officers, below the belt? I am sorry for that; but I am not going to change my words.

Can we change the situation for our and for our wards safety?

This article is dedicated to all the parents who send their children to the schools and for school buses in time or before time.

Chapter: 23

Miser or economic

Let me start with a story of a great man, may be, it is a story of Bernard Shaw, (as told by my mother, when I was very young) the famous English writer who once supposedly refused to take Nobel Prize.

His nemesis always branded him as a miser. The story goes like this.

Once, he was approached by a group of young people at his residence for asking for a donation for a library. At that time, he was in his study room, reading a book using two candles. As soon as he was approached by the group, he put off one candle and started discussion regarding setting up the library and how he could help in their efforts to set up a good library for the young generation. When the group asked for a donation, without uttering a single word, he gave a cheque with a reasonably good amount which made the group awestruck.

Then, one of the youth dared to ask the great man with due apology, 'Sir, when you put off one candle for our discussion, I thought you are not going to give a single pound as donation for our library, but--.'

Then the great man replied, 'I am an economical person, not a miser. When I was reading, I needed two candles, but when we were talking, light of one candle was sufficient. That is why I put off one candle. So far donation is concerned, you people are coming for an honest and good cause, as a citizen of the country, and I should contribute as much as possible.'

His exact sentences may be different from what I am writing here, but I am trying to convey the essence of his version. He not only saved his money by limiting his needs but also try to conserve energy and also reduce pollution at his disposal.

But sometimes, when we try to emulate the actions of those great people, we become laughing stock among our own peers. How?

Let us take one such example. Suppose you are provided a lunch packet in a meeting, which is much more than you can consume in one go, what you are going to do? If it is India, most of us will do a mess of the rest of the food articles after consumption, which will be no more eatable for anybody else. But if someone amongst you, neatly pack it and put aside for future consumption, many of us contract our eye brews and stamp him as a 'miser' or so.

Of course in many European countries, I am told, anyone is not allowed to waste food even if he/ she pays for it. In some countries one may have to cough up a hefty amount as fine for wasting any food.

But it is also true that there is a very thin difference between miserly person and economical person. Particularly when we say about ourselves, we call ourselves as 'economic' and when we talk about others; we call them as 'miser'.

Ok, enough of serious talk! Let me share a story of a very senior officer who retired long back. I do not know whether he was a miser or economic, but after reading this story about him, you may be able to decide in which category he should be placed.

At that time, he was heading an organization and therefore, he had to attend a lot of meetings, and many a times he had to attend more than one meeting on the same day. Naturally, sometimes, lunch was also served in those meetings.

On that fateful day, he had to attend two meetings and he was informed that lunch would be served in both the meetings. He instructed one organizer to send his lunch to his room so that, he would be able take the lunch with the other party (keeping the other lunch for his dinner). As instructed, the lunch was handed over to the personal peon of the senior officer for safe custody.

The personal peon, out of curiosity or otherwise, opened the lunch packet and ate the banana from the lunch packet and again packed the lunch packet neatly. After the arrival of the boss, the peon handed over the neatly packed packet. The boss opened the packet and found the banana was missing (as he already enquired from the organizer what are the items packed). I am told that there was a 'Mahabharata' (Bitter fight) between the peon and the senior officer which was witnessed by many of the officers and staff working under him. Please do not ask me in which group I have put this gentle man, in the group of misers, or in the group of economical persons or in a special group, as suggested by you.

This article is dedicated to all economical and miserly persons.

Chapter: 24

Alter Ego

I am narrating a borrowed story of sacrifice of a modern middle aged man to his loved one in the context of typical 'me too' case of a famous journalist.

A middle aged senior officer in an MNC, started loving one of his juniors. He expressed his desire to marry the girl without imposing any authority to accept his proposal. The girl politely refused. But the officer could not but stop his love for the girl. However, one day, he called the girl and assured her categorically that, though he was still in love with her, she should not worry for her refusal and he would help her if she would need it, both at personal and professional life.

After few months, the girl got a better opportunity and required a certificate to the effect that she had been a good worker in the post she was holding. She approached her boss quite hesitantly, as she was not sure how the spurned boss would react. But to her surprise, without slightest hesitation, the officer gave her a certificate which can only be given by a father figure to a junior officer.

The girl left the company and joined the other office located in a different city.

After two years, the man got an invitation letter for the marriage of the girl. In between, there was no written or verbal communication between them. The man could not attend the marriage due to his preoccupation, but he did not forget to send a gift and a bouquet of flower on the day of marriage.

Another one year passed, without any contact with the girl.

After more than one year, the man had to visit the city where the girl used to stay on an official visit.

It is a cheer coincidence, while coming out from a restaurant, he met the girl and her husband, who were about to enter the restaurant. After, initial introduction, the couple invited the man for a cup of coffee. Though he was in a hurry for another meeting with a client, he obliged.

They talked for more than an hour on different topics like best of the friends were meeting after a long time. However, to their utter shock, before they could finish the coffee, few terrorist struck at the restaurant and the man died on the spot while shielding the couple from a barrage of bullets.

The middle aged man sacrificed his life for the girl whom he loved but was spurned by the girl.

The story did not end there. The girl got shock of her life, when she was informed that she was going to inherit properties of few crores as per the Will of the man. Incidentally, the man was unmarried at the time of his death (as he had to sacrifice his marriage for the parents and younger siblings who were initially dependent on him and left him in lurch, once settled).

Apparently, the middle aged person was a saintly person. But it was not exactly that. He was all along thinking to have that girl for his own good only. He was always praying, the girl should not be happy with her husband, so that, she would come back to his life. He even thought, if her husband would die, he would have a realistic chance to marry that girl. Therefore, he all along wished that, either her husband should leave the girl voluntarily or he should die untimely. But when there was a realistic chance to get rid of her husband, he saved him by sacrificing his own life.

Why he did that? Can he be condemned for his ill thought? As per our religious book, only thinking a bad thing, unless you execute, does not invite punishment from God. Almost similar line of thinking prevails in our judicial system.

(The story is based on Panchatantra and Tal Betal, where the merchant is replaced by a Senior MNC officer, Paricharika is replaced by subordinate officer and Dasyu by terrorists And finally it is clarified, the story is based on some unconfirmed facts).

Chapter: 25

Taking advantage on someone's death

This is a story of deceit, revenge and molding a tragic incident to own benefits. It is a story of 1960/ 70s. It is a story of a young widow whom everybody blames, but I could not blame her after knowing the story from her perspective.

This young lady was married to a Government servant at a tender age of seventeen. Just after marriage her husband got a transfer to another city which is far away from his earlier posting at his home town. The husband, being the only son of the parents, kept his newly wed wife at his parental residence and joined at his new place of posting.

He applied for his transfer, but he did not get it till his death. I am told that, at that time, the officer who was at the helm of affairs for the whole country, was one of the most unsympathetic officer, the concerned department ever had.

One year had passed and no transfer was made for the poor fellow. He applied for his transfer again and again, but his transfer requests had been rejected on different excuses. The day, he got the last rejection letter in response to his transfer request, he committed suicide by hanging in an orchard adjacent to his rented accommodation.

As a knee jerk reaction to the suicide, there was lot of hue and cry to attend all the pending transfer cases in the department at the behest of the so called tough manage master, the departmental head. Lot of pressure was built up from the employees' union (including political) and the administration succumb to the pressure and all the request transfers were acceded. The poor fellow became a martyr for his fellow employees who were applying for their transfer to the place of their choices.

His close friends knew that he did not commit suicide because of the official letter he received on that day, but for the other letter which was also received on the same day. What was written in that particular letter?

A few days earlier, the poor fellow got a letter from his mother, congratulating him that he was going to be a proud father. He was very happy on that day. But heaven crashed on him when he got that particular letter from his wife where he was categorically informed by writing that she was not impregnated by him. In his absence, the brother in law of her husband, raped her (it is her version, others differ and many blamed her) and she became a victim of an unwanted pregnancy. The very night he committed suicide, not able to bear the deceits from his near and dear ones.

The wife did not share the pension benefits with the poor man's parent as she believed that for her misfortune, parents of her husband are equally responsible along with their son in law. Others painted her as loose character and heartless.

I do not know who is correct and who is wrong in the consequential situation. But I squarely blame the son in law as the main culprit of the whole unfortunate episode, who betrayed the social fabric of a family, his own wife, his own brother in law and his parent in law, by having a sexual relation with the wife of his own brother in law. I also do not want to have a debate, whether it was a consensual or otherwise sex with the wife of own brother in law. Whatever may be the situation, the brother in law of the victim cannot be condoned for his illicit acts with a very young and inexperienced married lady, that too with the wife of the younger brother of his own wife.

I also condemn actions of those friends who took advantage of the tragic incident for their own benefits (transfer to the places of their own choices).

Chapter: 26

Divorce

A few years ago, a friend of mine confided to me something which I am going to share with you in detail with his tacit permission with only a caveat not to disclose his name, organization he was working and also the place of working.

He was around 50 and working in a reputed organization at higher level. He has been known to me for the last three decades and I know him as a suave, impressive and with a very handsome personality. He was a father of two college going children and husband of a very beautiful wife. I knew him as a successful man, a doting father and a dotting husband. His wife was also a charming, but very dignified looking lady.

What he confided me was a rude shock for me. According to him, he was very faithful till he completed his eighteenth. According to him, his wife, who was very soft spoken to others, was actually very foul mouthed lady to her husband and to the children. She was a very bad cook and worse house maker. Despite of this, he tried his best to harmonize the marital chord up to the maximum. Though, he was suffering silently from within, he tried his best to adjust with her as much as possible. However, he thought, he was fighting a losing battle over the years.

Just after, completion of his 18th anniversary, he had to visit a city which is infamous for night club etc. In that tour, he met another old friend who took him to a place, which he had never visited earlier.

After that visit, whenever he visited that city, he made a habit to visit those place(s). Even after that, there was no immediate problem he had to face in the family front. However, he lost interest in his wife and rather he loved to avoid her.

The problem started in the last two years when he confided his agony to me. He met a girl, half of his age, not very beautiful, but soft spoken and who cared a lot about him. Initially he ignored that young girl, but subsequently he also became close to her.

'Where she is working?' I put this question, doubting that she might be working under him.

'She is working in my office, but not working under me.' He told me.

Then I could understand, why, all of a sudden, he told me that, his wife was foul mouthed and he was not loved by his wife etc. However, some of the allegations he had made, I agreed considering the fact that, sometimes his wife retorted him without any provocation from him. But whose wife does not do it?

'Are you sure she (his new love) loves you?' I asked him.

He said that he was not sure about that.

'Then why do you put yourself in such a situation where you may lose both of them!' I asked him.

'In any case, I don't want to continue my rest of the life with my wife (he actually used another word). I started hating her and I have tolerated her enough.' I smelt hatred in his voice.

'What do you think about your grown up children? Further, the young girl may file a case against you for sexual harassment, if you pursue her after her refusal (assuming that she may refuse his proposal)'. I gave my opinion as well, put a pertinent question.

'I shall give everything whatever I have, to my children and wife and want to restart my life afresh. So far the girl is concerned, she has given me all indication that she loves me; like coming to my cabin without any work and sharing my meal from same plate etc. Even if the girl refuses, then I shall not pursue her. Even after that, if she files a case, as you said, I shall confess that, yes, I love her.'

'OK, what do you want from me?' I asked him.

'Convince my wife to give me divorce.' He requested me with folded hands.

I said a damn no to him. I told him, that I might request his wife to be more compassionate to him in future and should restart their life in a more matured manner with due respect for each other. I also told him that, they should sit together for some time and ponder where they went wrong. They should continue their life in such a way that their children should not suffer due to fault of their parents.

In the meantime, I came know that, some of their relatives were also involved in inciting both the parties. Though, his wife did not want a divorce, she did not want to reconcile also.

I wrote about this in my FB, so that, I could convey this message to his relatives (at least one of them was my face book friend) to help this couple to be united both physically and mentally, so that, their children do not face undue stress.

Unfortunately the couple could not stay together for long; they divorced with mutual consent. My friend married the young lady after two years of their divorce. I heard that the relatives who had instigated the wife of my friend for divorce had never visited the lady after her divorce. Surprisingly, the children also preferred to stay with their father and their young step mother.

Chapter: 27

A positive message on failure

Why we should not worry for a failure in life? Many people have many strong reasons for that. I have my own!

It all started when, during a standing tea session under a tree outside our office premises, I commented that, one should not worry for a failure when one of my most favourite junior colleagues, was worrying for the result of an examination where he had appeared.

I explained my version of reasoning: If one has to fail 100 times in his /her life, one failure means, 100-X(x number of failures already suffered)-1 which is always less than the number, which otherwise, number of expected failures. Therefore, one should celebrate on his/ her every failure in true spirit.

Another, favourite colleague, said, though that is true, it is very difficult to digest a failure.

In my opinion, one should digest the pain also, if possible, enjoy the pain. It will give you the opportunity to learn many good things about life including the true meaning of friendship and many bad things of life including exposure to the true colours of pseudo well-wishers.

'It is easier to be said than done'. My colleague argued.

'I also fully agree with you, but one should cultivate the habit to tolerate these pains to be a successful person in the life. It needs lot of practice to acquire the ability to digest the pain with a smile.'

Then I told them about a meeting with a classmate few years ago.

"I met a classmate, after twenty years in a café without any prior engagement. We both became very happy to see each other after a long time. She said, after having some conversations, 'you have not changed over the time.'

I told her, 'I might have also changed, but not as much as you have observed changes in our other friends. Probably, others have changed more.'

'Probably, for you everything is fine, compared to others.' She observed.

'May be yes, may be no.' Then, I listed out some of my failures compared with my friends/classmates/ batch mates in the last twenty years.

Then I told her, 'Even when, many of my classmates/friends/batch mates got something good very easily and I could not get those things even after my best efforts, they showed unhappiness about the system whereas, I seldom condemn the system. Again when I got many bad things in my life/service when none of those classmates/friends/batch mates of mine did not get any of those bad things for their better luck, they still envy for my hearty laughs. Many of them, apparently, less happy than I for no apparent reason.'

'I would be happier if my husband is also like you!' She heaved a sigh.

I told her, 'Please do not expect that from your husband. Rather you try to become like me and be happy.'

Hugging me she told, 'Yes, you are right. I shall try to follow your path of happiness."

After finishing the story of our meeting, I told them (standing members of tea sessions), 'I do not know whether she followed my suggestions on attaining happiness or not, but I can assure you, I always try to follow my life like what I have said to her. I am always trying to do what I am advocating (at least in this respect). No matter, I do not know how much I am successful in my efforts.'

I know, I am not a very successful man in life; but can everybody be successful in life? On the other hand, with little effort, everyone can have a hearty laugh no matter he is successful or not in his life!

Chapter: 28

I Enjoy Your Company

It is a universal question, we often posed to ourselves, 'If you/ he/ she/ they have not come to my life, what would happened to me?' If my parents were not there, I would not have been here, to write this narration. For my parents, life would have been different, had I not been there. Once somebody comes to your life, even if he or she leaves, memory remains and you ask/tell yourselves, if he/she had not come to your life, you would be better/worse off than today.

Normally, when we utter this phrase, we, characteristically, refer to our better half. But, in reality, the person whom you may refer, may be anybody (except your parents, because your very existence is causal of your parents), may be your children, may be your spouse, lover, colleague, classmates, batch mates, neighbors, friends, foes and so on.

You may ask me why I have put your foes in the same bracket with your friends. In my opinion, both friends and foes have equal impacts in building your character and in building your career. If you see some historical personalities and mythological personalities we club both in the same bracket. For example, Ram-Ravan, Durga-

Mahisasur, Hitler-Mussolini-Churchill and so on, are pronounced in the same breath.

Few years back, I lost one of my first cousins in a tragic way, who was only 29 (for me, he was more like a nephew as his father was only few years older than I). Sometimes now we think, if he was not there at all, we need not have to get that shocking news at all. Again we think, there are so many good memories of him that, he may still alive with us, at least spiritually.

A few years ago when one of my friends lost his young daughter (whom I had never seen), must have the similar feeling. There cannot be any appropriate words which could have consoled their losses, but I am sure, same feeling of emptiness hovers over them with the same question.

Sometime, even small interaction may have long lasting impact. As a personal experience, a few years back, I met a fifteen year old girl while travelling by Rajdhani Express from Guwahati to Delhi. The girl boarded at Kanpur and narrated her story of her grief which was fallen on her family one month back prior to our meeting.

Her father, working in a PSU, was returning from Kolkata to Delhi after attending a meeting. The train does not have a regular stoppage at Ghaziabad where his residence was. The train slowed down, immediately, the fellow thought that, if he could get down at Ghaziabad he would save two-three hours of un-necessary travelling time. He got the brief case and got down from the running train, which might be running at a speed of around forty km/hour. He lost control and had a head injury and succumbed to his injuries after five days. But before his death, he could tell the story and he muttered again and again, 'why I wanted to save that 2-3 hours journey time?'

That is perhaps destiny for that poor fellow! However, whenever, I travel by train or any of my near and dear travel(s), I always narrate this story reminding them not to jump from a running train to save few hours of travelling time.

Had I not met that girl on that day, who knows, I may also commit the same mistake some time.

One of friends asked me a question, 'which types of husbands love their wives more?' He gave the answer also in the same breath, 'those who were spurned by many girls.'

Recently, I got a New Year message on my mobile, 'Agar tum na hote, mei kisko Happy new year bolta! (If you were not there, whom I would have said, happy new year!)'

Whether with a serious tone or with a lighter vein, we always ask the question to ourselves for a particular person, 'if he/ she had not come to my life, whether my life would be different or not?'

Chapter: 29

A Provocative Thought: If I die tomorrow

This thought comes to my mind from my very early age. It may come to minds of many of my friends as well.

Being dubbed as a bad/negative thought, we always try to brush aside this particular thought. But whenever I thought about it, I find many facets of human relations; some good some bad-but tolerable and some extremely unbearable.

I am sharing some of my thoughts (in lighter vein-but in reality, may be bitter truth) on this most disturbing issue when I was in the fag end of my career. Further, scenario, I am narrating below is not the same what I was imagining few years back when I was much younger. And I am sure, if I live for another few years from now, my expectation at my death, may be different from the list given below.

First reactions:

Wife and children: Shocked and no other immediate reactions except weeping/crying.

Close Friends: Shocked. No immediate comments.

Close relatives: Mixed Reactions, Some will be unhappy, some will say: 'Go to hell'.

Distant relatives: Is it True/ Very bad news! Matter ends there itself.

Friends: Very Sorry. Does my schedule allow me to go to Cremation ground or visit to his residence will be suffice!

Seniors in office: 'The rascal went with many unfinished work at his table-which will be my headache now!

Juniors (close): Unhappy. They will have gloomy face for the rest of the day.

Juniors (not close): Whom I have to report from tomorrow? Will my new boss be better than the deceased boss?

Acquaintances: Very bad news.

Scorn Enemies: Good news. But the B... should suffer a lot before his death. How that B.. can die so peacefully!

Persons whom I have to pay: How I shall ask back my money from his wife!

Persons who owe me: I should return the amount. But even if I do not return, what will happen?

Persons whom I promised (jokingly) to pay half of royalty expected to get from my books, after 17 years: Sir to bhag gaya (sir ran away without fulfilling the promise) with a grin!

After two days:

Wife and children: Busy in narrating the same story again and again to the visitors, how I have died. Smile and laughter have come back to their faces. Busy to discuss whom to invite for the rituals and what are the items to be served.

Friends: They will explain to my family, particularly to my wife; what are the benefits my family would get from my office. They will also offer to help if necessary.

On the day of Final rituals:

All will be busy in relishing the food and are generally happy with a get together within (outside) office hours. If lucky, some marriage proposals will be discussed about my and others' children.

In the evening, my family members will take a stock of the situation and discuss about the attendance of the relatives and friends in the 'death ceremony'.

After one month: Wife and children will be busy in visiting the office for family pension and other benefits. All other will be busy in their own works/duties.

After one year/ two years: All pension benefits are settled.

Wife will say, 'I alone cannot organize Annual (If I am lucky, first ritual will be solemnized without any hitch) ritual ceremony, and you people are reluctant, so the idea has been dropped to hold Annual Adya Shradha ceremony in the coming years.'

And finally say a good bye to Hiranya Borah forever.

If, there is a system of looking back (If God allows), I shall realize, how fool I was in thinking, without me, they would suffer, and therefore, I should live till they are settled and if possible live longer and longer!

Please do not take an offence for showing the mirror of an ugly truth.

Chapter: 30

Punctuality

When I was posted at NSSO (FOD), my junior colleagues nicknamed me as 'Rajdhani Express' as I seldom reach my office late even by five minutes of the office time and leave office before time.

In my entire service career, probably I am late in less than fifty occasions of which ninety percent of the total late comings were beyond my control.

Is it because of my good habit or due to a genetically acquired trait? Probably, both are not true. It is because of a psychological fear in my sub-conscious mind, encrypted by a hanging watch of a Principal who happened to be my mother's controlling officer when I was hardly a five year old kid.

My mother, who was appointed as 'Head Pundit' (Head Master of a Middle school) at the age of 19, had to report to the Principal of the Normal Practicing School, Sootea on her transfer from Behali after her marriage.

As a rural daughter-in law, she had to do all her household chores including rearing of animals and husking of paddy etc. before going to school. Despite of her best efforts, she sometimes failed to reach the school, which was neat two kilometer away from our home, in time, by five minutes or even less. She had to travel two Kilometer on foot every day. But for her it was a short distance as she had to travel every day eight kilometers, one way, every day as a student. From a very tender age, may be two and a half years I, along with my elder brother, who was one year, three months' older than I, accompanied my mother to the school. I need not have to mention here that , there was no crèche facility at that time and maternity leave for a working lady in Government was only 2 and a half months. There was a large field in the school, where we used to play with animals and stray boys and girls who never attended school in those days.

Whenever, my mother was late, the Principal used to show his watch pointing towards my mother and some times, he murmured, 'what example, you are going to set before your young children?'

When, I was about five year old, one day, he invited me to his chamber and told me, 'I know, Your mother always try to come in time to the school, but she is not able to do it because she may not be very good in time management (probably, he said some other words), so when you will grow, be careful, so that, no boss can show the watch, he is wearing, for your late coming. Always try to reach school/college/office before your teacher/boss reach the class/ office. Then, only you can aspire for bigger success.'

Still, I remember his voice and his advice which had been encrypted in my memory with awe and fear. That is the reason, why I report for my duties before the designated time, as far as possible.

Further, keeping in my mind, the plight of my mother for attending school and household chores, I am always, sympathetic to all my subordinate young mothers and so far, I am yet to scold any young mother for late coming for which, many a times, I get flaks from my seniors and male colleagues of those young mothers. But, I am still helping the young mothers as far as possible and I think, that is the only way to show my token of respect to my departed mother.

The article is dedicated to Shri Abani Bhagwati, B.Sc. (H), the then Principal, Sootea Normal Practicing School.

Chapter: 31

Who Never Enjoys Life

The people who are always fearful about their own death cannot enjoy their life fully. I know many may disagree to the above statement. But, let me start with my own experience from another popular topic.

At least, everybody will agree that, ghost stories sometimes terrify many people. Therefore, many people avoid hearing ghost stories at night. I was admonished many a times by my relatives for telling ghost stories at night. In my childhood days, I always liked to see the fearful faces of my brother, cousins of my age whenever I started a new ghost story. Frankly speaking, I have a strong desire to face a ghost to ask some questions. But alas! I am yet to come across any of that kind so far!

Once, Yudhisthir was asked by Yama, 'Kimacharyam (what is the most surprising philosophy of life?)? His answer was well known, 'everybody knows all living creatures have to die one day, but everybody thinks (in an illusion) that he/she will never die.'

In my early days also whenever, I talked about my own death, my parents and other senior relatives used to give me a good dressing down. But I liked that. A years ago when I posted similar thought on FB account, all my well-wishers jumped to conclude that I should not be a victim of negative thoughts. I really respect their concern and I sincerely thank all of them for their love shown to me. Probably, I would also have reacted similarly if any of my dear one posted such type of narration.

Then, why I am harping on the same issue?

Take the instance of the Ghost Story for once again. Who do not want to hear ghost story at night? Answer is clear, those, who are fearful of Ghost. Similarly, who do not want to talk about his/her own death? Those, who are fearful about own death- which is unfortunately, inevitable. Death is inevitable, only timing is different for different people. Then why do we avoid discussing own death? Death gives gloom to others; but not to the dead person. In reality, dead person attains eternal peace. Then, why we fear for death? Probable reason may be, we do not know, what is after death. Nobody is sure about that. That may be the crux of the fear for death!

I used to enjoy my life fearlessly till I get married and losing my courage steadily as I crossed some milestones of my life. After my marriage, I became fearful of my own death thinking that, what would happen to my wife. Then after becoming a father, I became more fearful about my own death thinking about my family. I seldom discuss about my own death, as if, if I discuss about it, I would die soon. Silently, I calculate, my DCRG amount etc. to know whether that would be enough for education of my children or not. Those are the days, when I was engulfed with negative thoughts and fear for death which prevented me from enjoying my normal life.

But thanks to the Almighty, one morning I realized, I should not bother about my own death as the same is not in my hand. From that day, I started to live my life again for me. I am not saying that I stopped worrying for my family. Yes, I do worry for my family, but without worrying for myself.

Those, who know me closely for years, they know that, at the dead of night also, I am not fearful to go out all alone, if duty warrants. Even for social visit or for having pure fun I never mind to go out at the middle of the night all alone, not only in known places but also in completely unknown places, within and outside our country.

That is the reason, those who travel with me to some places, after their return, complain to me, 'I also could have accompanied you, had I been told (by you)!'

But who will tell you? You have to take chance and risk to enjoy something/ to know something! Ruing for the lost chances will not help, dear friend, muster the guts to abandon the fear of taking risk.

Again, I am cautioning you that, I am not encouraging you to jump before a train or a water fall to taste the unknowns. I always advise my juniors to take calculated risk to enjoy life. For example, one of my colleagues did not accompany us in a voyage to a lake, where thousands of tourists visit daily. Even, he discouraged some of our junior colleagues not to undertake the voyage. Unfortunately, one of our junior colleagues taking his advice did not accompany us who repented later on.

Similarly, when I requested one of my friends to accompany me to a Plaza after office hours in a city of a foreign country, he refused to accompany me, citing bad law and order situation in the city. Actually law and order situation in that city was far better than Delhi. On the next day, he asked me, whether I had visited the Plaza or not. After my affirmative answer (knowing that I was not attacked by any hooligans-I do not know, whether, he would be happier, if I would have been thrashed) and when I told how beautiful it was and returned by midnight after shopping, he rued for the missed chance, as in the next morning, we had to leave the city for Delhi.

So my dear friends, if you want to enjoy life, break away from the stranglehold of 'Kimacharyam' (what is the most astonishing feature of life).

Chapter: 32

Misuse of English language in Public

'Bhaiya B-30 kaha Parega, Pandara Road (Where is B-30)?' Few years ago three young boys, about 19-20 asked me in Hindi when I was carrying two heavy bags to my residence after alighting from the metro at Khan Market Metro Station, New Delhi.

I told the direction to the youngsters. I did not mind, though I am not 100% sure, if my ego was not hurt, when they addressed me as 'Bhaiya', a derogatory address for a well-educated person like me. However, 'bahiya' is also used to address an elder brother within the family members. In this particular case, they did not address me as their elder brother, as in reality, I may be even older than their parents. But I was not angry with them; rather, I was amused that they might have thought me as a labourer. Oh! Please do not tell me that they thought me little older than them (Should I not be happy!).

Though in those days, I was new to that place, I had already noticed, that normally, there are very few pedestrians on the streets except daily wage earners, CPWD's manual workers, students and family members living in the Servant quarters. Therefore, their address to me as Bhaiya, not as uncle or something else, might be perfectly justified. As, in India, Dignity of Labour is the first causality in the public places!

But what followed had disturbed me a lot more. All three boys appeared to be from good family background and that was really worrisome. They were walking about five feet ahead of me and thinking (probably) I am illiterate, they freely, with pretty loud voices, were discussing about a common friend, using the dreaded four letter(F...) word quite frequently, ignoring very existence of an old (or young) fellow like me. There may be two reasons of ignoring me, one, they might have the perception, that I am an illiterate person or, two, they don't bother, very existence of any other fellow, irrespective of his age, background etc. The second perception is probably more dangerous.

That reminded me an old incident involving one of my school teachers, Late Chota Mian Sir, who taught us English in class VIII. He was an extremely simple, but very learned man and on principle, he never used to wear any shoe or chappal on his feet and always clad in Dhoti and Kurta.

The rail way line connecting Tezpur (Rangapara) and Jonai (North Lakhimpur) is crossing a village named as 'Ghahi Gaon' in Sootea Subdivision of Sonitpur District of Assam. Sir used to take a short cut to school which was along the train line.

One fine morning, he saw a crowd on the train line. When he approached the place where the crowd had been gathered, he saw a tom- tom car with two railway officials on it. They were inspecting the track. But reaching the place, he was feeling very bad as the two officials were talking in English and criticizing the crowd in a derogatory manner. After listening to them for few minutes, in chaste English, he asked the officials, should he translate to the villagers what they were saying about them (villagers).

For a moment, they were shell shocked and in the following moments, with folded hands, they apologized for their words and requested Sir, not to translate what they were saying about the villagers. Sir did not translate those sentences, but advised them not to repeat the same mistake in future.

I am sure, they never repeated any such type of mistakes in the rest of their lives.

I told this story many a times to my children, so that, they do not underestimate any person by looking at his dress or on the basis of background, colour or any other reasons.

Let me come to the original point. If the present generation develops a feeling that, anything can be spoken in public by using English language, we, as guardians have the bounden duty to impress upon our wards to see the reason, for not doing that again!

However, in India, unfortunately intelligence of a person is judged by English speaking capacity. It is nothing but a colonial mentally inherited from the British Raj in India. I am blessed to visit a few non-English speaking countries where progress in industrial sectors and other scientific sectors are far ahead of India or any other South Asian countries where English is spoken amongst the elites. We normally conveniently forget that English is nothing but a language to communicate our minds to another person like any other language.

However, I agree that English is a lingua franca for most of the countries in the world; but it is also equally important to remember that English is not the most spoken language in the world!

This article is dedicated to Late Chota Mian Sir.

Chapter: 33

Departure Terminals vs Arrival Terminals

Few years ago, while coming from Kolkata to Delhi one question struck in my mind, 'Why Departure terminals are always (exception may be there, but at least all the terminals, I have so far visited) above the Arrival terminals?'

After pondering for the right answer during the entire flight from Kolkata to Delhi, I have found few answers:

1. You are excited to fly, so you can climb up at the time of departure, whereas after arrival, you are tired enough to climb up.

2. At the time of arrival, you are grounded to face some ground realities.

3. Sky should be nearer from departure terminals.

4. On arrival, you have to do lot of works, including fighting with Auto/taxi driver, so you must have a strong foothold.

5. At the time of departure, you may get two wings thinking about beautiful faces on board, therefore departure terminal is above the ground.

6. You may get your wings clipped after possible beautiful faces on board turned out to be most disgusting and foul mouthed one sitting beside you and therefore you are already suffering from a very low esteem syndrome. To symbolize your mood, arrival terminals are placed below the departure terminals.

7. Always unseen is more beautiful than the seen one.

8. You may have high expectation from your co-passenger before your departure.

9. You may have high expectation about on board flight refreshment at the time of departure which may have already been completely demolished at the time of arrival.

10. Before your departure, you may expect that, flight will be on time, at the time of arrival, you forgot the original expected time of arrival.

And so on. Please let me know, if you know the real reason of constructing departure terminals above the arrival terminals.

Chapter: 34

D-School

This piece of thought (monologue) came to my mind, when a senior, who was well known for his ego, gave a lecture to the newly recruited officers on how to become good officers in a function on a foundation day of an institute.

After hearing his bombastic lecture, I have decided to open a school after my retirement, where I shall teach youngsters how to become good officers. To achieve my goal, I shall invite all good (?) officers to deliver their lectures to my students.

To qualify to deliver lectures to my students, I have decided that the following qualifications would be essential for the lecturers:

1. He should have good personality and he should be fluent in English (grammatical mistakes are tolerable).

2. He should be a limpet in either senior officer's room or should always try to make friendship with only better service (than his own) people. For example, if he is from allied service he should try to make friendship with only IAS/IPS, no matter, how the other person thinks about him.

3. He should never say, 'Hello' to any of his junior officers, unless he is greeted first. But he should relax this condition for beautiful lady officers.

4. He should expect all files marked to him by his subordinates, should be 100% in order so that he can simply sign and forward to his boss; because he has to be busy in going to senior officer's room or to his newly acquainted person who belongs to a better service.

5. From his parked car in the office premises, he should not carry even a small article to his office. He should call his peon to carry the article. But he should not be fussy to carry a large suitcase full of articles of the daughter of his boss, studying abroad while on a foreign visit. After all, he is getting the opportunity for going abroad, is not based on his merit, but for licking the boots of his boss.

6. Since he is a very good officer, he does not need any training in any part of the country (unless his son is studying in that city). But if the training is organized in foreign country for lower level officers, he should convince his boss (otherwise what is the use for taking PRC (permanent resident certificate) in his boss's room) that he is eligible for that training and that will enhance his capability to handle important issues.

7. He should be MCP (Male chauvinist pig).

Salary will be negotiable depending upon some desirable qualifications as stated below:

1. He should not work in the office unless there is some benefit he expects.

2. He should be ready to issue a memo to his juniors at the drop of a hat.

3. He should be ready to touch feet, if he is in trouble, to anybody (even to the junior to whom he had issued a memo on the previous day).

4. He should always try to show off his big ego at any place, any time!

I may add any other qualification on the advice of some of the lecturers who would be already selected!

Chapter: 35

Demi-Goddess

I was attending a seminar on 'terrorism and murder of humanity' in a particular city of a particular country. I do not want to mention the name of the country or the city deliberately as the contention of the story is independent of country, city or any race.

Participants were asked to share experiences of facing terrorism of any form in their places by self, by relatives or by close friends or by their community. Since I hail from a place where terrorism had shown its ugly face in the late eighties and early nineties of the twentieth century, I raised my hand immediately for sharing my experience.

'Terrorism started in our region in the late eighties. Unfortunately, very few families had been unscathed from the menace of terrorism. Practically we may find only a select group of people, who had not been effected by the brunt of the socio-political conflict engulfed in the entire region. Taking advantage of the volatile situation, a group of disgruntled youths were misguided by local vested interest intelligentsia and also by few unfriendly neighboring countries to take the path of terrorism.

The youths, who took up arms, they became blood thirsty day by day and killed many innocent persons across the region irrespective of caste and creed.

One of my brothers in law who tried to mobilize people to stand up against the terrorist group was killed by the terrorists in broad day light. Ironically, a few days after the death of the poor fellow, a cousin of mine, who happens to be a terrorist, was also killed by security forces in an encounter.

That shows, from the same family one was killed by terrorists and another member of the same extended family was killed by security forces for being a terrorist. It was not clear, whether the slain terrorist had any link with killing of my brother in law. That may be ugliest face of terrorism!' I stopped there.

Many participants had shared their tragic experiences with terrorism. But one of the participants' story made everybody in the room shell shocked and there was pin drop silence for few moments as none of the participants had the guts to break the silence.

After getting my wits back, I stood up from my chair and went up to the participant and hugged her with tears in my eyes.

Her story in a nutshell is like this:

She was a lecturer in a local college and husband was working as a doctor in a Government hospital and was also as a project officer for eradication of communicable diseases in a district. He was a very devoted doctor and his motto was 'service to mankind is service to God'.

One day, he met an eight-year old girl whose parents were killed by a group of terrorists on some flimsy grounds. He brought the girl to his home despite of resistance from his friends and relatives. He wanted to adopt the girl as his own daughter. His wife also reluctantly agreed to her husband's proposal. After fulfilling some formalities, they became the legal parents of the orphaned girl.

After that, the doctor along with his professional work, started a crusade against terrorism. This angered the terrorists and they warned him to desist from his efforts to make a strong public opinion against the terrorism. The group issued warning of dire consequences for not heeding to their warnings. But the doctor did not stop his crusade.

One morning, when he was going to drop his sons, one 10-year-old and the other one 12-year-old, at school, the doctor was abducted. Despite of presence of more than thousand parents and children, none came forward to stop the abduction bid, though incidentally, some of them were patients of the doctor. Even after the abduction, none of the parents came forward to give clue to the police in their efforts to rescue the doctor.

After three days, the wife got a call from the abductors asking her to come with one million (in terms of Indian currency) rupee to a secluded place. With great difficulty, she arranged the amount and handed over the amount to the emissary at the place selected by the group. She was given another address, where she was told that, her husband had been kept for the last three days. She hurriedly went to the place.

At the assigned place, she saw a car without any driver or any other person in it. When she reached the car, she found three black big polythine packets were kept on the floor of the car. She saw a letter was attached to one of the bags. She opened the letter with trembling hands. In the letter, it was written, 'Your husband was too heavy to carry in one piece. Sorry for the inconvenience.'

That ends her story of grief.

After, the end of the programme for that day, all the participants went to their respective hotels. After, taking a shower, I went for a walk in the adjacent park.

From a distance, I saw the lady was walking aimlessly. I approached her and greeted her which she returned with a polite smile. I wanted to know something more about the incident; beyond she had told in the seminar.

I started my conversation with a cautious approach, as I did not want to hurt her sentiment by asking some questions which might again remind her those terrible days. After, a little conversation, she became friendly and asked me about my family etc.

Without asking, she told me that, her elder son was pursuing medical science and younger son was doing para medical at that time. The adopted daughter, who was indirectly responsible for her husband's death, had been her only companion for the last eight years. They complimented each other in their days of sorrows.

'Now your problem days are over, hopefully!' I commented.

'Yes and No' She thoughtfully answered.

She narrated the present situation in her country after her personal tragedy occurred eight years back.

'Gradually, the terrorism faded from our area and culminated with surrender of the leader of the terrorist group after three years. He publicly submitted an apology to all those families whose members were killed by the group. I also got an apology letter from the group leader for their inhumane acts. My adopted daughter also got a separate letter of apology.' She paused for a minute. I did not want to disturb her any more.

She again started, 'In the meantime, the Government took lot of steps to rehabilitate the victims of the terrorist attacks/ atrocities during that time. My two sons were sent to an advanced country for their studies at Government expenses. I became a much-respected lady amongst all, as my husband's sacrifice led to a strong public opinion against the group, which completely alienated them from the mass public. Finally, the terrorist group had little option left, other than performing a surrendering drama.' She again stopped.

'Now, everybody thinks, I became a demi goddess. I am invited for talk show as a wife of a devout crusader of peace. I am treated like an ideal mother and widow of a martyr of peace, but I am not a woman of flesh and blood. They think, I do not have any humanely desire- I am a doll made of earth or plastic, no personal feeling, a woman normally should have.' She looked at the sky after finishing her story.

'Everyone thinks I should live with the memory of my late husband. But I know, it is impossible for any lady to live only with the memory of her late husband. Every third day, I also feel the need of the company of a male on my bed.' She told me looking at the lamp emitting deem light in the park.

I had noticed lot of anguish in her voice which was piercing my heart like a spear. I could not find any word to heal her anguish and pain.

I kept mum for a while so did she. After a long silence, she asked a pointed question to me, 'Can I stay in your room for the night?'

I thought for a while. I understood exactly what she wanted by asking a simple question. I saw in the dim light of the park; a bright face is waiting for an answer.

'I have no problem in inviting you for the night, if it makes you happy. But you should think twice before staying with me for the night. Afterwards, you should not repent by lowering your status from a demi-goddess to a mere mortal.' I cautioned. I indirectly tried to dissuade her from taking a decision which might have many repercussion in her future life.

'You are worried for me or for yourself?' She asked me with a faint smile. I saw lot of sadness in her voice.

'Ok, Come and stay with me. Hope you will enjoy my company. My room number is 209 at the second floor. Probably we are staying in the same hotel.'

She gave me a broad smile for the first time.

I took a shower for the second time in that evening to become fresh before arrival of the visitor who was willing to stay for the night.

When I was drying my body by wrapping a towel as the only cloth on my body, I heard the soft sound of knocking on my door. As expected, she was standing at the door. Before I could invite her into my room, she gently pushed me away and entered into my room. She was wearing a red gown. For the first time, I realized, she was beautiful and maintain an extremely good figure at an age of forty plus.

'Would you like to take a cup of tea?' I asked her.

'I can.' She said softly.

I was about to dress before preparing a cup of tea for her. But she had a different idea, 'Please do not put on formal dress now. You are looking extremely good with your towel.'

On her request, I did not put any more cloth on my half naked body. When I offered her a cup of tea she looked at me as a street beggar waiting for a meal. She touched my chest with her beautiful hands and said, 'I have seen a bare chest of a male after eight long years.'

'I shall try to make you happy tonight.' Clasping her hand, I told her. She did not say anything.

After three days, when she finally said a good bye to me at the airport, she appeared to be very happy. I did not see any sign of repentance on her face. She said a departing sentence, 'We may not meet again in this life, but I shall cherish these three days and nights for rest of my life!' She smiled again with a clear sign of happiness on her face.

I felt a little bad for my wife.

Chapter: 36

Daughter

For the last few years, Kanak realized his strong fondness for a young girl who was few months younger than his only son. His wife and he had a feeling that the girl would be good for his son who was working in a multinational Company as a senior Engineer. He had asked neither the girl nor his son about the possible alliance. As per his information, none of them were engaged to someone else. Then where was the problem?

The girl always used to refer to his son as 'Bhaiya' (elder brother) and his other siblings as sisters. One day Kanak asked the girl, why she was referring his son as "Bhaiya' she answered, 'Since I regard you as my father, your son will be my brother only.'

She was correct in her arguments and therefore, Kanak also reconciled the fact that she would not be his daughter-in-law. So respecting her wish he started to consider the girl as his own daughter.

But to make a girl 'own daughter', who is not blood related, having her own parents, is a very tough proposition. We generally opined to a girl of our daughter's age that, 'you are like my daughter!' in a very loose manner. We must understand one fact, there is a big difference, between telling a girl, 'like my daughter' and to think or to consider a girl, as his 'own daughter'.

What is the chemistry between a daughter and a father? Father is the first and last male in the life of a female who can sacrifice everything, for her without expecting any return from her. He is the best motivator in her life and ultimate well-wisher for her. For her, he is neither male nor female, neither god nor goddess but still everything for her till she attains a certain age. After crossing certain age, father becomes the best friend, next only to the mother, to whom she can confide almost everything, even her problem of stomach upset to stomach pain before and after menstrual period in absence of her mother. At different age, her perception about her father changes, which is basically need based.

But the perception about the daughter never changes over time for the father. Basic perception about the daughter when she is one day old and 30 year old does not change. For example, when a daughter embraces his father at the age of five, the feeling remain same, when daughter is 25. But same cannot be said about another girl. Similarly, if one's daughter is not wearing sufficient cloths in winter, the first and only reaction will be, 'cold should not catch her' which follows a scolding with an advice to wear a sweater or a jacket. At night, in winter, father goes to check whether his daughter is taking blanket properly or not and in summer, whether speed of the fan is perfect or more. He checks in daughter's room at night whether mosquito repellent is properly working or not or the net is properly inserted or not. But similar actions you cannot take in the room of a 'daughter like' girl, as she may think otherwise. Even, you may not have the same feeling about the other girl.

Therefore, to consider, a girl as your own daughter, a lot of real acclimatization in your thinking process is needed. It is real tough.

Is it same for the girl who may think you as her own father? In a sense, it may be tougher for her in some of the aspects and easier for some of the other aspects.

Let us think for the easier one first. She can expect all the facilities what other daughters are getting from their fathers, both physical and monetary. She can claim also those earthly and emotional things for her comfort or otherwise. But what's about her faith on the man, whom she tries to accept as her father? Whether, the man is pretending as a good man, but actually he is nothing but a shark? Take the same example once again, will the feeling remain same, when the daughter embraces the new father at the age of 25 and when she embraced her father at the age of five. But if feeling is not the same, then she is yet to be 'own daughter' of the new found father. Similarly, if the daughter finds her new father at night, roaming in her room, checking whether she is taking the blanket properly or not, in winter and in summer whether speed of the fan is perfect or more, how will she react? Can she discuss her personal problems with her new father with same ease, as she does with her father? If yes, only then, she can have another father, at least at par with her own father.

So far Kanak is concerned, as soon as he is mentally prepared himself for acceptance of the girl as his 'own daughter', he will give her permission to call him as, 'Papa/Daddy/Deuta'. But he will never pressurize the girl to accept him as her father. She can take her own time to take her decision and Kanak will wait for years together to hear her decision, may be till he gets his final call from the above.

After taking this important decision, Kanak became a relived man.

Chapter: 37

Sacrifice- Damn it

Two friends met after twenty years. After, exchange of pleasantries, they started talking about empowerment of women.

First friend boasted, 'With same intelligence and ability, because of her duties towards our family, my wife has to sacrifice a lot.'

The second friend agreed to his friend's observation and asked, 'Anyway, what sacrifice she had to make for your family?'

'During her first pregnancy, she had to turn down her promotion, as she was posted outside the city on her promotion. Finally when our second child was born, she had to resign from that lucrative job and settled for a teaching job which is much less paid and career-wise, it is nothing compared to the earlier job.' He explained in a tone of sympathy and genuine sorrow.

The second friend with a mischievous smile answered, 'Your wife's sacrifice is nothing compared to my wife's sacrifice for our family. She had to sacrifice a most sought after job, which was never offered to her. She had to sacrifice her most decorated academic career, which is nothing but a modest one, lest to say. Even she had to sacrifice breakfast...'

'She is not taking breakfast! What do you want to say!' the first friend astonished.

'No, no my friend, she has sacrificed the satisfaction of preparation of breakfast for many years. She had sacrificed the satisfaction of cooking for lunch and dinner on non-working days. She had to sacrifice, all the useless talks on dining table for hours in their mother's house.' He smiled wearily.

'Do you mean to say, she is not doing any work?'

'I have not said that. She criticizes me and my family members all the time. She even does not spare my parent who left this world long ago. She says, except her, nobody works at home. While cleaning the kitchen, she always criticizes, that I spoiled the kitchen while cooking. According to her, in the office I am doing nothing except chatting with my friends.' He concluded.

The friends departed wishing all the best to each other. Both were thinking alike after departing from each other. Each of them was thinking, 'what an expert I am becoming in lying in telling about my better half!'

Actually all the wives may fall in the limits the two friends had drawn in their over-emphasized statements. The first wife was not that good what her husband had boasted about her and the second wife was also not that bad what her husband had told about her.

Chapter: 38

Am I Kanak

Some of friends are repeatedly asking me who is Kanak (the protagonist in many of my articles). To satisfy them, I am introducing Kanak in the following paragraphs:

Kanak is articulate, amicable, aristocratic, arrogant, acrimonious, actor, brave, beacon, benevolent, brutal, betrayer, bigot, capable, clever, constructive, cool, courteous, cunning, corrupt, childish, childlike, coward, critic, committed, compromising, dotting, diligent, decorated, dare devil, dogmatic, dominant, deceptive, dramatic, demonic, draconian, destructive, demonstrative, deep, educated, energetic, enterprising, elusive, fiery, fighter, friend, fighting fit, fussy, ferocious, funny, guide, god fearing, good looking, humane, helpful, hardworking, hard ball, hilarious, honest, independent, intelligent, idiot, joyful, jovial, jaded, knowledgeable, loving, loyal, lusty, lamenting, limpet, learned, manly, mannered, matured, molded, moderate, misunderstood, nurtured, naughty, non-negative, nuts, non-committal, outspoken, ordinary, out layer, positive, proud, prompt, punctual, patriotic, philosopher, philanthropic, photogenic, purposeful, queer, respectful, resourceful, religious, revengeful, romantic, rustic, rascal, smart, smiling, suave, selfish, spiteful, stupid, shallow, trustworthy, truthful, underscored, underestimated, understanding, virile, victorious, vocal, vibrant, venomous, warrior, wily, wealthy, womanizer, xenon-like, Xeroxed, Zoomed, Zebra-like person. These are A to Z attributes given to him by his friends and foes.

Oh, I am sorry; you are still not sure, who is Kanak?

I am Kanak/ We all are Kanak /You are Kanak/ He is Kanak / They are also Kanak at different time and at different situation. Kanak is with full of qualities, some positive, some negative and some are in between. He is my guide, philosopher and friend who never ditched me and never abandoned me. He follows me like a shadow. He is like a hen hovering over her chickens. That is why, I love Kanak.

Chapter: 39

Penance

Kanak met Amit after two decades. Kanak was two years' junior to Amit. Amit's character and behaviour are diametrically opposite to that of Kanak. Amit is a 'my dear man' to all his friends and relatives and Kanak is neither 'my dear' nor suave enough to talk politely to others. Kanak is blunt and only popular to a select few group of people. But despite of diametrically opposite in characters, Amit loves Kanak due to his frankness and bravery. Due to this elder brotherly love, Kanak respects Amit like his own brother and once picked up a fight with a senior when he referred Amit as 'Maiki (Female/ village woman)'. In due course of time, Amit joined civil service and Kanak was employed in a regional bank as an executive.

Amit was very happy to see Kanak unexpectedly in a Mall on GS Road, Guwahati.

After exchange of pleasantry, Kanak asked about his family. Amit told his two sons were in IIT Delhi and pursuing engineering in mechanical and computer science.

'That is great! You must be a proud father!'

'Yes. But credit goes to your Bau (Sister in law) for the achievements of the children. It is her Tapashya, what makes them so good.'

'How?'

'I was posted at Tezpur for six years as ADC (ADM) when my children (they are twins) were admitted at Tezpur Don Bosco. Then, I was transferred to Dibrugarh on promotion as DC (DM). But my wife did not accompany me for the sake of the children and stayed back in a one room apartment till my sons cleared HSLC. Again, she shifted to Guwahati to accompany the children when they were admitted in Cotton College for higher secondary. After admission, she stayed in a two room apartment with the children, till they were selected for the undergraduate courses in IIT. Now they are in hostels and my wife started staying with me after a gap of eight long years. Therefore, I give all credit to her (my wife) only.'

'But, Dada, you have also sacrificed a lot in the process!' Kanak opined.

'Yes, a little bit. But compared to her, those are nothing. During her absence also, I need not have to cook nor do any domestic chores. But without any servant, she had to do all domestic chores including cooking even when she was not well. That is real sacrifice.' He concluded.

Now, Kanak understood, real meaning of Tapashya. In Mythology, he read of Tapashya of the Munis (learned persons/ sages) to achieve something. In the present context, he learnt about modern Tapashya. He imagined the sacrifice made by a lady, who disassociated the comfort of a wife of a DC (modern king of a district) for the sake of the career of her children. He also understood why he failed as a father and for that matter why his wife also failed as a mother. None of them sacrificed anything for their children. As a result of that, Kanak's children are doing pati (most ordinary) BA (graduation in arts subject without honours/ major). He thought his children's future will be as bleak as of his own.

Chapter: 40

Lovely Gifts

Kanak got two gifts from two lovely ladies; both were strangers few hours before handing over the gifts. Both the gifts were given to Kanak as token of love and appreciations by the ladies of the same age when Kanak met them for the first and last time in his life. Kanak is yet to come to a conclusion: which was the better one between the gifts he had received few decades ago.

It was a normal tour for Kanak, when he was posted in a field office at Guwahati in 1992. He was returning from a small city, Silchar of Assam to Guwahati by Barak Valley Express.

If any of my friends who visited that place, would know that, the train service from Barak valley to Brahmaputra valley was one of the most un-enviable train services available in India during 1989-2015. Normally, it takes 24 hours to cover 394 KMs, practically with no facility in the running train. It is free for all and particularly, without valid ticket passengers are most welcome persons for the corrupt railway staff.

Kanak had a valid AC-II tier ticket and occupied the allotted seat well before departure time. From his window, he noticed a very beautiful young girl escorted her mother towards his bogey. A few minutes later, the lady occupied the only other seat in his coupe and asked him whether he was also going to Guwahati. After little conversation, he came to know that, the lady was also going to Guwahati after dropping her daughter at the medical college hostel, Silchar for the first time. After half an hour the train started at the right time, 9 AM and TTE came to his seat after another half an hour to examine Kanak's reservation status. The lady requested the TTE to arrange a seat in the female coup for her. Kanak also did not mind at her request as he was also not comfortable in sharing the same coup with an unknown lady. The TTE assured the lady that, he would try his best to accommodate her request.

The train was moving at a snail's pace as expected. As there was no alternative, both of them were talking on different topics, ranging from official to politics and politics to family matters and so on. They took lunch at a small station and had a nap for an hour or so. By 4 PM, darkness descended in the hilly track.

The TTE came to the cabin and told the lady, if she wanted, he could change her seat to another four seated cabin where a family of three was travelling. The lady thanking the TTE told that, she was no more interested to change the seat.

After dinner, the lady told Kanak that, being a diabetic, she had to go to toilet more than once in the night, so he should not mind if she put on the dim light throughout the night.

Kanak told her, 'You may consider me as your younger brother, therefore you need not request me for anything. If you want something from me, you just tell me.'

The lady quipped, 'Long ago I consider you as my own brother, otherwise, being a lady how I could have dared to share a coup with you for the night.'

In the next morning, Kanak got down one stop before Guwahati. The lady gave two oranges as parting gift, saying, 'You give two oranges to your children saying that their Jethai (elder sister of father) has given to them.'

Kanak never met that lady again, but he thinks that, those two oranges are one of the best gifts he has ever got from a stranger.

After that incident, Kanak encountered another experience and received a gift from another lady whom also he had never met again.

Kanak was on a tour to a metropolitan city a few years back to attend a national seminar (may be in 2004). The seminar was attended by participants from all over the country. During tea break he noticed a lady of his age trying her mobile phone repeatedly, but, apparently not getting any connection. Kanak asked the lady what was the problem. The lady said that she was trying to connect his son and her father to tell that, she reached the metropolis safely. Kanak offered his phone, from which the lady could connect his son and her father instantly and conveyed the message. The lady thanked profusely Kanak for the help. The seminar started again and during lunch time again both of them talked on different topics.

For the lady it was her first visit to the city. When Kanak told her that, the city was visited by Kanak earlier also several times, she requested him to accompany her for shopping. Kanak hates shopping with a lady as he feels it is a boring and thankless job. However, he could not refuse the request of the newly acquainted lady out of courtesy.

After the seminar, both of them went for shopping and during that time Kanak came to know that the lady was abandoned by her husband when she was pregnant due to some dowry related reasons. At that time, she was not having any economic resources to support herself or to her child. With great difficulty she managed to get a job after compromising many issues. Even for getting the present job, she had to physically gratify the Chairman of the selection committee. Kanak felt very sorry for the lady. He knows that, it is not one off example in our society.

After dinner, at around 11 PM Kanak dropped the lady at her hotel and then he left for his hotel.

Again, in the next morning, he met the lady in the seminar in a very jovial mood. She told Kanak that, she would not attend the session after lunch as her train would leave at 3 PM. During the lunch time, she handed over a small replica of the town hall and a piece of paper. She told Kanak, 'This is a very small gift for you, for taking the pain to accompany me to the market. You read the piece of paper inside the envelope after I leave the venue.'

Kanak thanked her for the gift and as promised, he opened the envelope only after the lady left the seminar hall.

It was a small hand written letter with very neat hand writing. 'Thanks for the company in my shopping yesterday. I have met many persons, good and bad during my struggle to afloat in my life. Those who helped me in my struggle, either they are my close relatives or they expect something financial or physical favour, even for a small help. Those who know my pathetic story, even without providing any help, try to exploit the situation. But, you are the first person in my life, who helped me, accompany me for more than four hours, but did not try to take advantage of my background even though you had sufficient scope for that. You dropped me at my place at the middle of the night (11PM) even without touching my hand. I am very much envious about your wife. God bless you and your family.'

Even after so many years, Kanak could not come to a conclusion, which gift was a better one, from a stranger!

Chapter: 41

Pain of the First Kiss

A few decades ago, during a Bihu (spring) vacation, Kanak visited his maternal uncles' place. That was a sleepy town, but during Bihu it comes to life due to Bihu Mela (Cultural functions organized during the Bihu Festival-Assamese Cultural month from 13th April to 12th May). In those days, the Government used to declare around 15 days' holiday for all the Government schools. Taking advantage of that, Kanak used to visit his uncles' place during Bihu time.

Kanak has a cousin, Babloo two years' older than him. At that time, he was a real naughty rascal. He used to tease each and every girl of his age contrary to Kanak's character of respecting all ladies of all ages. In his entire life he never teases any girl except those who are very close to him. Kanak used to carry a reputation of a very good boy in his own village as well as in his uncles' small town.

During the mela, Kanak used to accompany his cousin to different places. He also attended functions at night with him. In one occasion, while he was enjoying the programme, he noticed, his cousin slipped out of the venue of the function leaving him alone.

On the very next moment, a young girl, of his age sitting just in front of him started scolding him, 'You stupid, why you people come to cultural function? Just, for molesting girls?'

Before Kanak could realize what had happened, another girl told the annoyed girl, 'No, he is not the culprit. I saw Babloo, who ran after doing the dastardly act.'

The girl immediately tendered an apology for her behaviour and asked him who he was. After his introduction, she said, 'I know about you. My father used to say lot about you. But your cousin is a short of rogue. Do not be with him. He will spoil you.'

Kanak did not say anything. But he silently recalled his father's advice contrary to general advice, 'Stay with both good and bad friends. You can learn good things from both. Always try to pick-up only the good things from a bag filled with both good and bad things, like a swan who drinks only milk separating from water. Further, no swan dies of cold, no matter how cold water is.'

Two days after the incident, his youngest uncle took Kanak to his friend's house who happened to be the father of that girl. It was evening time and as usual there was no electricity due to unscheduled load shedding. Therefore, like most of the rural households of India, lantern was used as a stop gap arrangement in that house also. The father of the girl was known to Kanak's parents. As uncle and the father of the girl were talking, the girl escorted Kanak to her study room.

The room was neatly kept with one small bed, a study table and one chair. The girl let Kanak to sit on the bed and she also sat nearby. She asked Kanak whether he was still angry for her behaviour two days before, as without verifying the facts she scolded him.

He said, 'No, but I was little bit puzzled at that time and I was short of words.'

The girl told him that she knew him by name, not by face for the last few years. Kanak expressed his surprise to hear that he was known to a young lady of his own age even before meeting.

The girl explained, 'Sukanya, from your place is a friend of mine. She told me that you are the first boy of your class; you represent the school in the school tournament in debating, extempore speech and recitation competition. Even once, your one act play, directed by you got the best director's award in the inter-school tournament.'

Kanak was highly impressed with the girl for her informative knowledge about him. 'And you see my fate, when we met, without your fault I scolded you!' She concluded.

After some more tit bits, the girl asked him, 'Do you love somebody?'

It was a straight question which he never heard from any girl in his life. Kanak murmured, 'No.'

The moment Kanak said no to her question, the girl kissed Kanak on her forehead and then on his cheeks and finally on his lips. Instantly, with an impulse, Kanak embraced the girl and kissed her all over.

After a minute or so, the girl pushed him away and said 'Someone may see us!'

On the very next moment she left the room. After a few minutes, Kanak also left the room and joined his uncle.

He could not sleep whole night and he was thinking the whole episode again and again. After two days he left his uncles place but could not erase the memory of that evening.

During summer vacation, his cousin visited his place. From him, Kanak came to know that, the girl was sent to a boarding school at Guwahati.

Because of shyness Kanak could not ask his cousin about her anything more than what his cousin told as a routine update on the girls from his locality. He even could not ask the name of the school.

Time passed. Initially, Kanak used to think about the incident every day and slowly thinking about the girl became rarity.

After HSLC, he left his home for his higher study. At first, he went to Guwahati and then to New Delhi. In due course of time, he had almost forgotten about the girl till his cousin told him that the girl was married to a Dentist working in a small town near Guwahati.

But, after a year or so, a news about the girl devastated Kanak to the core. The girl died during her first delivery. Doctor could not save both mother and son as the mother has O- RH negative and the son in her womb had B-Rh positive. Kanak could not sleep for few days after receiving the news. He felt a void despite of the fact that, he did not love the girl nor has any opportunity to meet her in his life for the second time in an intimate manner.

Kanak felt disturbed by recalling that lovely incident. He questions himself, 'Did she love him? Or she also forgot him as he did? He could not have an answer till today. But whenever, he is alone, still he feels wet lips of that young girl, his first kiss from a miss and feels a deep pain in his heart. He met the girl only twice in his life but no girl has a lasting impression like her, as she taught him how to kiss a miss!

Chapter: 42

Swimming Lesson for a Village Boy

It is not about me, how I learnt swimming, but it is about all those village boys who learnt swimming as a necessity rather than an exercise or as a sport.

When I was in primary school, I used to go to school with my mother. But as soon as I reached class IV, I have to change my school and therefore, my school time and holidays differed slightly with holidays of my mother. That gave me the opportunity to roam around the village and go to the nearest river. The nearest river, situated on the western side of our village, Mornoi, as the name suggest, is a killer river which is infamous for her killing spree during summer, the season which starts from April and ends in the month of October in Assam. The second nearest river, Ghiladhari situated on our east, is a larger river, with a lesser killer instinct, though one of my cousin drowned when he was about 10 in that river.

My father was a good swimmer. He took us (me and my elder brother) to Ghiladhari to teach us the basics of swimming for 2-3 days. But due to his preoccupations, he could not concentrate on us and left to our own efforts.

During this period, whenever our holidays did not coincide with our parents, we used to sneak into the flowing water of the nearest river along with our friends. To learn swimming, river is a better water body in a sense that, if river is not in full flow, there may be some patches where the river is deeper than the other places. So you may start at the deeper place, even if you do not know swimming, with little bit of guts, little bit of gulping of water, you will reach the sallow area because of the current of the river. We started learning swimming in the river with the help of current of the river keeping in minds the basics that our father taught us and with the help other friends.

However, one day, I was about to be drowned because of my misjudgment about the stretch of the deep water. Still I vividly remember those few seconds when I left all hopes of my life till one of my friends pulled me out of water by catching my hair. I still remember, when he put his hand on my hair, I thought that, it was the hand of the Yamdoot, as I heard many times that Yamdoot used to pull the dying person by catching his hair.

Anyway, I was saved and from the next day I never faced such situations in my life. In due course of time, I learnt all types of swimming. Unfortunately, the boy who saved my life on that day, died in a tragic circumstances a few years later (not by drowning).

During my period of learning, my mother was very much against about our going to the river due to her fear about the river that has a fearful reputation. Therefore, we used to go to the river without informing anybody and without taking any extra cloths. All of us, used to swim in our birth day dresses in the river or any other large water bodies around our locality. In the process, we could know each other's anatomy very well.

Now, I realize why we call our childhood friends as 'langotia yaar' (friends who know others beyond under-garments) because we cannot say as 'friends with whom I roamed even without cloth' or 'birth day dress friends' etc.

This article is dedicated to my friend who saved my life on that day.

Chapter: 43

Birthday Thought

I wrote this article on my 53rd birth day. Nothing much has changed in my life since then except my retirement.

"Before I express my thought on this D-day, let me thank all my well-wishers who wish me 'Happy Birth day' on my unimportant B-Day'.

I am also thankful to those friends, who have not formally wished me on this day, due to different reasons, but who always stand by me during my difficult days. I also express my gratitude to those persons, who made me look the world differently. I shall also remain grateful to those personalities, due to whose actions, made me tougher and stronger.

Today is a different B-day for me for many reasons. Earlier, I have never been given a bouquet on this day. Thanks to the young brigade of Social Statistics Division, Ministry of Statistics and Programme Implementation, I got one today. I have never gotten any opportunity to cut a B-Day cake earlier but- today I got it. Again, thanks to the young brigade. God bless them! This is the first time, when I got some good wishes from across the border also. This is one of those B-Days when none of family members is with me, no doubt, their best wishes are with me as always.

Many of friends asked me what would be my programme tonight. I told them, I would write a long post. One friend advised me to write a short one as none has the time to read a long post. My wife also told me once, 'Probably nobody reads your post, why are you wasting your time in writing those useless craps?'

Recently, another friend told me that they have lot of better works to do than writing such a long post. I fully agree with him. I do not have any proper satisfactory answers for them. But I am trying to find out the answer-may be because, I love to write, when I want to convey some message to someone, instead of telling him/her directly by uttering some words. Many people have already accused me of being foul mouthed and many could not understand my words due my rustic pronunciations. Many of my friends/ colleagues mock my pronunciation in my absence also.

But today, I do not want to put myself in any controversy on those issues.

On every B-Day, I recall the whole year and try to find out how many good work(s) I have done. Then I want to add up the good works done in the last so many years after attaining the age of 10 or 12.

I do the similar exercise for bad works as well. Then, I try to find out the number of routine works in a similar fashion. Let me share my findings with my friends who are able to read up to this line:

Good work: - Last year- Nil, entire life-3

Bad work: - Last year-10+, entire life-500+

Routine work:-Last year-100+, entire life- 5000+

My life is dominated by routine works and followed by some bad works. Some who reads my post up to this line may be interested to know as per my definition, what is a good work.

As per my definition, a good work is an action through which I helped one or more persons without iota of selfishness. Even I should not have any expectation, for a mere 'thank you' while performing those works. The last good work, I have done, probably long 10 years back.

Then, what is a bad work as per my definition? Whenever, I got a chance to do a good work, but I avoided with an excuse, that is a bad work. I need not have to say, bad works include, any action which causes physical, mental agony to a person or a group of persons including my own family members, friends, colleagues, deliberately or otherwise.

A routine work is any action(s), which has either no consequence to the general public, Government, friends and foes or very little consequences to others. In this category, I also include those actions, through which I expect accolades, thanks from the other parties, whom I helped through my position or otherwise. I also include all positive actions for my family, extended family, friends and my colleagues in the category of routine works.

I know, many will differ my definitions of these qualities. It is quite natural. Reportedly, even definition of mother tongue has been changed eleven times over the censuses in India.

I shall definitely try to improve my tally of good works in the coming years and for that I need blessings from all of you.

Before I conclude, let me ask you, 'How many good works you have done in your life as per my definition?' I am sure, your tally of good works will exceed mine.

(Even after posting of this FB post, my tally of good works has not exceed from mere three.)

Chapter: 44

Director, Mr. X or Mr. X, Director

Power corrupts and absolute power corrupts absolutely. But how one can become powerful?

If you can reach the top of the organization/ government/ company, automatically you will be powerful. How can one reach and stay at the top for a long time?

Unless you inherit the top position, you must have a trait (which I shall explain later on) along with competence and intelligence. Because your, competence and intelligence with your peers may be almost same, may be even less; therefore you must have specific trait. Then, what is the specific trait you must have to reach the top and become powerful?

'You have to lick the boots of the seniors, boot the juniors and cut throats of the peers.' This is a famous statement by a famous General, President and a Statesman of the world.

In administrative language, it is called ruthless, disciplined and loyal officer/worker/person/soldier etc. Once you are at the top, you are the master of all you survey, you are the judge and you're the chief executor. If anybody dares to challenge you, you just annihilate him/her.

But normally, technical people are not coming in this category. But always exceptions are there. A few years back, I attended a golden jubilee celebration of a technical organization at New Delhi. Retired top officers were also invited for the function. As soon as a retired top officer entered, everybody present there, rushed to him to greet him. This officer had retired about ten years back, but still commanded respect among the juniors. The officer could not only recalled everybody by name, but also knew about the family members, their problems, both solved during his time and even those unsolved problems during his time.

At least another ten top retired officers were also present in the function, but none was swarmed like him. No doubt they were also greeted by many of us.

But I noticed, another retired top officer was sitting all alone, nobody was talking to him. I, out of sympathy, went to the old fellow and introduced myself and asked, 'Sir, May I know, why you are sitting all alone?'

His answers perplexed me. 'Young man! Why you are talking to me? If any of your seniors see you talking to me, they may be unhappy with you also. Perhaps you do not know me, I am Mr.—'.

As a newcomer to the organization, I was told about this gentleman. When he was in the helm of affairs, he terrorized all the employees working under him, in the name of transfer, disciplinary actions etc. At the drop of a hat, he suspended many young officials. That was the first time I met this tyrant face to face. I surprised to see fear in the eyes of once most feared person. I understood that, he might be worried thinking, he might be humiliated by anybody, whom he had mentally tortured when he was in power.

I asked him politely, 'Sir, would you mind if I ask you a question?'

The old fellow replied, 'I know, what you want to know. No, I am not a happy person now. My misdeeds are now haunting me. Every day, I think why I did those acts. I sometimes, feel like committing suicide. But probably, God also does not want me. As an old man, I want to advise you, never think power will always be with you.

Power is like a prostitute, when you are on the top, you are the master, the moment you leave, and you are no more even concerned to her. Even if you have choice between, your career and your conscience, always go with your conscience. Never compromise your dignity and principles. I did realize this fact of life very late. I learnt it very late that, love and respect cannot be earned through enforcement of power and authority, it comes through your actions and virtues, mutual respect and cooperation.

I was a good man till I occupied the top post and power took over my head. Now, I curse the day when I was selected for the post.'

I observed that, his voice was trembling and eyes became moist.

A few years back I was presiding a farewell meeting of an officer who had a Topsy-turvy career. However, he was a very jolly person and he could mesmerize the audience whenever he used to speak on any topic.

After giving thanks to the organizing committee, he started his farewell speech as follows:

"I joined the service in --year and completed 35 years of a chequered career without any complaint about anybody who worked with me as senior or as junior. In my entire career, I wanted to be a good human being, rather than a good officer.

As an officer I am a total failure in the eyes of many of my seniors and I am a very good officer in the eyes of many juniors of mine. However, I must be grateful to all my 35 bosses except five bosses, in my long 35 years of my service career, who were kind enough to support me in my office work and for them only I am able to retire as ----.

You may be interested to know about those five officers, who gave me some torrid time during my career. Out of five officers, three were extremely good people and you all know, good people have to leave this sinful earth early; they also left the world of sin, well before their retirement.

Out of the rest two, one was sent to jail for few months by the authority due to some malpractices and the last one was allegedly beaten up by a junior officer, in his office chamber itself. When both of us were working under him, he used to instigate the young officer against me. Though, I had no role to play in all these happenings, both the living officers accused me as the chief architect of their misfortunes. Some accused me as unlucky mascot for my bosses. As a matter of fact, none of the officers died, when I was working under them. Similarly, both the incidents occurred about the living officers, well after I left those offices. But, I cannot stop anybody who had a bad opinion about me.

But I can tell you, out of other 30 bosses, one went on to become a member of the apex body of our organization, one retired as a very senior officer in UN, four of them retired as the topmost officers of the organization. Many of my earlier bosses also retired after reaching the second top most post.

But you all know, we always remember all the bad things in the wrong spirit. Some seniors termed me as rogue, who never listens to the advices of the seniors; some said that, I deserved to be condemned.

I always feel about those seniors (who were not having good relation with me) as they are innocent souls but lack of knowledge in the subjects dealt by us and administrative rules and regulations. It is the problem of the Indian system, where a person is identified by the designation, neither by knowledge nor by any other quality.

Suppose a person is holding the post of a Director, then he is taken by the society as 'Director, Mr. X, not as 'Mr. X, Director'.

These officers also think about themselves like that and treat their subordinates as their servants, not servants of Government of India or Government of a State. When they cannot argue on administrative points or technical points, they would say, 'you have to agree with me, because I am your boss.'

I never digested such type rulings in my life. I had always good relations with all the seniors, whom I thought, they are intelligent and hardworking and protective against any external pressure. I hated those officers, who advised you to do something and once it went wrong, he abandoned you like a mouse abandoning a sinking ship.

Many people may talk many things about you, but you and God only know what you are doing and what you have done. Therefore, I always do what makes me happy and in the interest for the country and staff working under me.

I may be implicated in things, which I actually had not done. Even the bosses know the truth, but they will never divulge the truth, because falsehood helps them. But God is always kind enough to me, whenever the bosses tried to harm me in connivance with some of the other senior officers, God rewarded me with something which otherwise, I would have missed in my life.

I am rather thankful to those poor bosses, for their misdeeds, I became mentally tougher and got chances to prove myself. Now I am a content man by achieving many things which, of course, may not be acknowledged by others. That is life. Even Pandavas who were protected by God himself, had to suffer entire life, so who am I, who would not suffer!

Always remember, sufferings are like fire, which give chances to get rid of impurities in your body and mind on regular basis.

I once again, thank all the bosses who helped me during my thick and thin and also those five bosses, three of whom are no more today, for their very good (Sic!) behavior /activities towards me, which made me mentally stronger, efficient and gave the opportunity to intellectually develop myself to some extent. I am also thankful, to all my juniors, whom I always treat them as my brothers/ sisters or sons/ daughters for their wonderful associations in my long journey. I also extend my.——"

After completion of his speech, I asked him, why he is so skeptical about some of his bosses.

Further, I asked him a pointed question, 'if I die tomorrow, you will make fun of my death also. Is not it, sir?'

'Yes. When, I said, the persons who die early, I really mean it, they are lucky people. They need not have to face humiliation in the hands of any junior whom he tortured mentally. Their very entities are associated with the posts, they were holding. They do not have any social status compared to even a person, who might have retired from a very low post. Death is the ultimate truth and ultimate escape route. Dead persons need not have to reply anything, good or bad. I also do not have any bad feeling about them. But, yes, it is a tragedy for their families; I have also full sympathy for them.'

Though, I could not agree with the retiring colleague in all the points he had made, he also tried to see his arguments from his point of view only.

I tried to compare the speech of the retiring colleague and the advice given by the retired person met on the golden jubilee celebration day.

Again I recalled of a person, who happened to be a nice person a few months ago, now fast changing to an authoritarian ruler after clinching a prize posting. I can see the future of the person, if his ego continues to grow like the way it is growing in the last few months, he may also end up with the same category of a person of the retired person, whom I met on the golden jubilee celebration day, many years back.

I thought for a while, whether I should talk with the person, whom I have lot of respect, not to allow power and authority take over his head. Being a junior officer both in status and in age, in a second thought, I desisted myself from doing so, because, if he does not take it in the right spirit, he may make my life also hell.

I also try to look back, as administrator, how many times I had to take tough decisions, which were not appreciated by many. Who knows, if I die tomorrow, my family will suffer no doubt, but many juniors/ colleagues may also mock about my death, publicly or privately.

After a sleepless night, I shrugged off all the negative feelings and surrendered to my destiny!

Chapter: 45

Without Telling a Lie

When are we not speaking the truth without telling a lie? Is it an art or compulsion? When we were young, our elders instead of answering some queries, they used to say, 'you will not understand now, you are too young.' They did it, may be due to avoid embarrassment or due to not having enough faith on us about our capacity to keep something confidential within the family. In office also, senior officers tell the juniors to leave the room to discuss on confidential matters. But in such type of cases, no articulation is necessary. It is as straight forward as the arrow of Arjun, which hit the target without any fuss.

But in our daily life, we cannot be that blunt. For example, you are going to enquire availability of vacancy in a tutorial class for your son and you meet one of your colleagues whose son is also in the same class of your son. On asking where you are going, your answer will be, 'I am going for an important personal work'. Here you are instead of speaking the truth, you are avoiding the question smartly, which serves two purposes, you are not blunt to say, 'Why should I tell you? Or I am not going to tell you.' Simultaneously, you are not speaking the truth without telling a lie.

After one week, when you meet the same colleague while dropping your son in the same tutorial class where your colleague's son is also taking class, you will behave normally and will not mention about the meeting that took place in the last week. Both of you conveniently ignore that, because your colleague also did not tell you when he had visited the tutor.

Take another example. Your super boss not finding your boss in the office, asks you about his whereabouts. Your answer is always between the truth and a lie, 'A few minutes ago, he was in his room.' The few minutes may be few hours also! After all, hour is born out of minutes only. Then, you telephone your boss secretly and will ask what to tell. Your boss knows that you are not speaking the truth nor telling a lie. You are excused by both the parties.

Those semi truths may be termed as your compulsion.

But sometimes we fear to speak the truth and do not want tell a lie. Take the example of some racial comments made by some antisocial to the people of another region of the country. We, instead of taking on the bull by horn, we try to say, 'it was not actually racial, it was perhaps a misunderstanding;' till a person at the top says, 'yes, it was'. This is a serious issue of not speaking the truth without telling a lie.

Even, in office, no doubt with lesser implications, we avoid to tell a subordinate about his short coming on his face. A few years back, some of the spineless officers used to give below bench mark ACR grading without informing the officer concerned. These spineless officers avoided to give adverse remarks which they are supposed to communicate otherwise. Even worse, some officers openly supported the juniors and instigate the boss to give bad ACRs to the juniors. Kudos to the honourable Supreme Court of India, for whose intervention, Government has to introduce APR system. Otherwise, rule of those spineless officers would have continued till date!

When a person tells about a girl who is junior to him in the office, 'she is like my daughter/sister', he is not speaking the truth or telling a lie. How? In extreme case, the man treats the girl as his own daughter/sister and that is why he loves her. However, in most of the cases, he cannot speak the truth mainly for two reasons, one he will be under constant scrutiny for every action towards the girl, whether he is biased towards her, and secondly, there may be resistance from his/her family. Therefore, he is taking the middle path. In the opposite extreme case, he is telling the statement to take extra work from her, while he may not have any iota of love for the girl as his own daughter. Since the officer does not have any ill motive also against the girl, one cannot blame him for the half-truth as age difference supports his claim. Further, he may think that claiming even brother-sister, father- daughter relation may adversely affect the performance of the juniors in office work!

Even when your two children ask you whom you love most, your answer may be like this, 'you both are like my two eyes, so there is no difference'. But truth remains, even both the eyes may not be equally good.

To conclude the story, the statements like, 'Always speak the truth', 'Truth always prevails', 'I hate lies', 'I always try to speak the truth', are good statements to hear, but they are also 'only half-truth'.

Do you agree whatever I have written above or not?

Chapter: 46

Paradise of a Fool

'Hi Kanak, how are you?' Looking back Kanak saw the person whom he loved to hate, Ranoj Das, one year senior to Kanak in his college.

Ronoj used to stay in hostel, though he was from the same city. When, he joined the hostel, Kanak was subjected to lot of humiliation at the hand of this senior. He not only ragged him, before the fresher's party, but also humiliated him many times due to Kanak's 'not so smart look', rugged dress and rural background. However, after one year, Ranoj had to join his class after dropping the final examination. Even in the second attempt, he could secure a second division only, whereas, Kanak managed to secure a first Division with distinction. Following the custom of the college, Kanak used to call him 'Dada' even though he did not deserve any respect. Even after cutting a sorry figure in the examination, he did not stop himself from humiliating Kanak in the slightest opportunity.

After few years, Kanak came to know that Ranoj was able to join category II state civil service and amassed lot of money by misusing his position.

With this background both met after 35 years. Ranoj has not changed in terms of physique as well as in terms of flaunting his status, higher than actual status. 'What are you doing now?' Ranoj asked Kanak with full of arrogance in his voice. Kanak replied what he was at that time with his usual voice.

'Oh, that means, you are holding much higher position than mine. But do you know, you, the technical people have to live with your salary, no matter how fat your salary is! Our daily income may be more than your monthly salary.' Kanak agreed by nodding his head.

Ranoj forcefully took Kanak to a costly restaurant, not because of love for him but to show his money power.

Let me reproduce their conversations in verbatim without any observation from my side.

Ronoj: Have you changed for the better, I mean in terms of dress, English speaking etc.?

Kanak: I do not know, dada.

Ronoj: Do you have a smart phone?

Knk: I do not have. I am not comfortable in using those. Further, I do not need it also. (At that time he did not have a smart phone.)

Rnj: One should be smart and good in English to do sms etc. in a smart phone. I know your English, so pathetic! Do you know, my son is also equally smart and good in English, like me? How (is) about your child (ren). By the way how many children do you have?'

Knk: Three, two sons and one daughter. Sons are not staying with us, at present, only my daughter lives with us. She is the youngest.

Rnj: You remained the same rustic village boy! Nowadays, no modern person will have three children, that too with a single income. You have spoiled your life as well as theirs. Where do they study?

Knk: You might be aware, that I married little early compared to others. Both my sons are working-only daughter is in school. Actually, between my younger son and daughter has a gap of 10 years.

Rnj: Is she studying in good public school?

Knk: No, all my children are (were) in Government school. Actually, I did not spend much on their study.

Rnj: Did not or could not? Your sons must be in private sector?

Knk: Yes. Both are in private sector.

Rnj: How much they are getting! 5000 Bucks or little more, Heh!

Knk: Elder son gets around 9000 bucks and younger one gets around 7000 bucks.

Rnj: That is exactly what I am expecting from you. Are you spending money on them till now?

Knk: No, now I am not spending on them. Forget about my family! How many children do you have and what are they doing?

Rnj: I have two sons and they are jewels in all respect. Like father like son. They are in very good public school. One is 18 and another is 14. But they are so intelligent; they can compete with any intelligent boy of 24. They can debate on any topic with anybody.

Knk: That is great! But, your elder son, being 18, how is he still in school!

Rnj: Due to his illness he could not sit in the last year's examination.

Knk: Oh, that is unfortunate!

Rnj: But you know, sometimes, more intelligence becomes a point of jealousy for others. Last time, a new teacher came and gave very less marks in English to the elder one. I called the paper, and saw, actually my son had done exceedingly well. But the teacher was like you, traditional rustic, who does not know, how younger generation writes in short. Cant' you follow? For example, you will write as 'How' but modern generation will write as 'Hw'. You will write 'modern', they will write 'mod'. Similarly, modern boy will write 'Gone to school', you old generation will write, 'He has gone to school' or 'he went to school' depending upon whether the time is mentioned or not. That old fellow deducted marks on those spellings and grammar. I told the principal, that either his marks should be increased or the teacher had to go. Then only, the teacher came to know that, every year I give a huge donation to the school. The teacher apologized and matter ended. Similarly, three years back, for missing few steps, my younger son was denied marks by the mathematics teacher. An extreme intelligent boy can calculate within his brain, what an ordinary boy has to calculate step by step. After these two incidents, I have decided that, after high school, both will be sent to USA, where people recognize the quality of intelligent people.

Knk: You are right Dada. If they will be sent to USA, the USA will be benefitted and India will lose two intelligent boys. Because, in India still in official correspondences, traditional English is used, they will not prosper here. Still we have to write notes elaborating the whole issues either in traditional English or traditional Hindi. Our boss expects us to write grammatically correct English as well! Hopefully, one day will come, when India will adopt SMS English! Then only, your sons should come to India to guide people to take correct decisions etc.

Rnj: I know the culture of the west. I teach them to grow like American. Their future lies there.

KNK: You must have visited USA many times and therefore you may have to teach them how their household chores do because in USA, they may not have servants and they have to do their own work by themselves. They may also have to share their apartment with others!

NJ: No I have not visited USA. You know, though I have lot of money, I cannot go to USA without permission of the Government. However, I know, doing household chores, sharing apartment etc. are applicable only for common people. I have sufficient money to fetch them.

Knk: That is nice!

NJ: You will see one day I shall be known for my children!

Knk: I hope too. But excuse me dada, I have some works to do, as I have to go back to Delhi tomorrow. Otherwise it is so nice meeting, we could have continued for some more time.

Rnj: I have also to go. Today, I have a meeting with the CM.

They were about to depart, at that moment they saw, a common friend Sanjay entered into the restaurant.

Sanjay is senior to Ranoj in the office, but otherwise, he was a classmate of Kanak. To see Kanak with Ranoj, he was surprised and greeted him with open arms. They again sat down and started conversation.

Sanjay: Both of your sons are in the same city, is not it? Are they settled down? When your daughter will go? Heard that, she has also got some scholarship!

Knk: So many questions in one go! Yes, both of them are in California and settled down properly. Daughter also got 50% scholarship from a college in USA. But she is not interested to go to USA. She is interested to go to UK for her graduation. But her brothers are bent upon to take her to USA. I do not know, what will be decided by her finally. After all it will be her life her future.

Rnj: About whom you are talking about?

Sanjay: About Kanak's children. Don't you know that Kanak's children are extremely brilliant, not like mine or yours!

(Based on true conversation between two persons-overheard by me, names are imaginary, mentioned service is also imaginary, little spices are added, characters are superimposed somewhat with some similar characters! I am Sorry for the character, Ranoj. There may be many such persons who live in a world of falsehood like, Ranoj lives for his entire life.)

Chapter: 47

Life or Dream

A friend asked me a few years ago, 'what is the ultimate truth?' I told him, 'I am living, and one day I shall die, for me that is the truth'.

'Even that may not be true!' He explained, 'Suppose, you are from a different world, where a person can live for more than 3000,000 years, whose one day is equivalent to 100 years. What you are feeling today as true, actually you see in your dream only. Whatever you see, feel revolves around you only. Therefore, very existence of everything living/ dead around you will depend on you only- so far you are concerned. Once you are awake, everything will vanish.'

I had no answer. Now, I also feel/realize in the same way. But if I think that way, I shall lose my appetite for doing any work which is against the very fundamentals of 'Gita'.

Chapter: 48

A Maid and Her Boss

When my close friend, Avinash, told me that he loves his maid, my eyes were about to come out of my socket. However, his love story is really a heart breaking one.

His maid had been working with his family for the last five years since his transfer to this city. The lady is working for another five to six families to meet her bare minimum needs. Every employer expects her to perform better than the other houses where she is working. She has to be on her toes for the whole day without any exception. She probably does not get a single sympathetic word from any one from dawn to dusk. Everybody thinks, she does not deserve the payment what they are making. Somehow, due to some unknown reasons, he started loving this lady and sometimes ears to her agony. Sometimes, he pays more than what his wife pays as per her monthly contract amount. Initially his wife was not very much happy about their relation. Now she has accepted their relationship albeit not very happily. Somehow, his children are happy about their relationship and they whole heartedly supported him, though sometimes tease him mentioning their relation.

What has attracted him towards her? He likes her indomitable spirit against all odds she has to face daily, for the last so many years. Her husband had expired 10 years before Avinash met her for the first time, after suffering from cancer for nearly two years. Her only daughter, aged 35 is almost bedridden due to polio. She has (should I use 'she had'?) two sons also, but after their marriages they left their mother and handicap sister in lurch. So this poor lady has to work round the clock to look after her daughter and herself at the age of sixty plus odd years. Due to his sympathetic attitude, she once said, 'Sir, you are a man of position, but it might be, in our previous life, you might be my close relative. God bless you!'

Frankly speaking, Avinash also feels, she might be some one very close to his heart, in their earlier birth. Is it possible?

When discussed the matter, he commented, 'one major problem in our country is that very few people value the services of the maids, cleaners, etc. for what they are worth. Think what would have happened to our big cities, if these people were not here to clean the houses and the public areas. Unfortunately, they are destined to live in slums and we don't want slums; but we want the slum-dwellers for our comfort! One has to realize that their services also need to be paid well. Remember that in the first place, they are here because of our need and due to their low wages, our lives become extremely comfortable. Therefore, when as members of a modern society, we shall start respecting the importance of their works and pay them accordingly; we would deserve to be called a part of civilized society.'

'Yes, well said my friend, I have no point of dispute on this issue.' I whole heartedly agreed to his points.

But immediately I recalled how 'our better half association' objected a simple demand for raising their monthly wage by Rs.50/- after implementation of our sixth pay commission.

Do you have any other points on this issue sir?

Chapter: 49

Do You Love Your Wife

If a person says, 'I do not love my wife' every known person will ask, 'why?' They may get similar and predictable answers, why that particular person does not love his wife. The answers would be like, because she does not understand his feeling in one extreme to the other extreme, she might be indulging adultery. You agree or disagree to his answer is a different story, but most likely the underlying content of the answer to different person is on the similar to those lines, in most of the cases in between the two extremes.

Normally, the question, 'why do you love your wife' is not asked. But if it is asked, most of the persons fumble to give an answer. Even he will try his best to find an answer which is very near to the truth, for his own consumption.

As a statistician, I tried to collect this information from a few friends a few years back. I am listing below different type of answers, I got from them. Some of them are very interesting, some are bizarre and some are really funny. My comments are given in the bracket.

She is the mother of my children (I also hope so).

She is the only person whom I can rely upon. (She must be a very efficient wife)

She is the person whom I believe most. (You may repent within a short time).

She is equal partner in my life. (What about your sins, which only your male friends and sinners in your arms know?)

She is a miser, I am a spender. Our combination is very good for our family. (You are saying, thinking financial benefits coming out of your married life. Is not it?)

She is earning, which is very much essential for running the family comfortably in this age of scarcity. (I found another wise chap on financial matters)

She is very good cook. (You could have married the a cook instead)

She does all the domestic chores. (You should better marry a domestic help, why you have married such an educated lady?)

She is very beautiful. (I shall always envy you.)

She is very sober and very polite. (You are dominating her personal life completely.)

She loves my family members. (You have already killed her emotions)

She is taking care of my family in absence of me. (You may be better off if you hire a Governess.)

Ours is a love marriage, therefore I love her very much. (Does it mean that those husbands need not have to love their wives if those were victims of arranged marriages?)

Do I love her? I do not know. (He is a totally confused person)

I am not smart enough to have any affair with somebody else. (Had he been smart enough, he would have not loved her.)

Can you suggest any other alternative? (He cleverly sent his ball to my court.)

I hate to love her. But due to social obligation, I have to love her. (You are facing stress for social compulsion.)

I have seen nobody is happy with their wives, somehow they are pulling. I am also doing the same thing. (A burden he is carrying, as he does not have a better choice.)

She is less nagging wife than my brother's wife. (What do you want to say?)

If I do not love, I fear she may run away with my neighbor's young son. (You should be careful!)

She is able to keep my neighbor's wife's mouth shut while arguing. She (my neighbor's wife) is very much abusive. (You have a genuine point.)

When she hits me, she always spares my vital organs, so that she can beat me again. (Thank God! You are still alive.)

She spares occasionally few pegs for me also after opening a bottle of whisky. (You are really a lucky chap.)

She is a dumb woman. Once, she caught me red handed with her younger sister. I told her that her sister is taking part in a drama in her college as role-model wife of 'Merchant of Venice'. She immediately apologized that she had not read that book, but she had read only

'Othello' of Shakespeare. (You will understand when your wife will take part in Mahabharata as wife of Pandava's.)

She came back to me after spending few nights with her new/old boyfriend. (You are great sir.)

Her father gave me dowry in monthly installment without fail till date. (Are you not afraid of jail?)

She can dance with all my friends in a party till she passed out. (I must say she is very social.)

She is very .....(no comments)

And so on.

My dear lady friends do not be against your beloved husbands for their not so palatable answers. I have done this exercise for ladies also to know the reasons behind for their divine love towards their husbands. Most predominant answers were 'love their husbands for social and financial securities given by their husbands', 'for welfare of their children', 'not objecting to shopping' 'apparently not looking eye to eye to any beautiful lady in her presence', 'not appreciating neighbor's wife', 'doing all the household works without any oomph', 'Every time I catch him red handed with someone else, he takes me to a Five Star Hotel for dinner or gives me an expensive gift', 'he is extremely rich', 'he is very energetic' and so on.(I have no guts to give my personal comments here).

So if you are in search of unconditional love from your spouse, then at least you have to wait for your next rebirth (incarnation). Till then, good bye! No offence please.

Chapter: 50

A Weak officer

Few years back, this question was asked by a friend of mine. I told him that, 'It is not limited to an officer only. When a person talks politely to a person of similar gender, the other person thinks he/she is weak. If a man talks to a lady politely, the lady thinks he is 'cheni' (a person having sugar coated tongue). If a lady talks to a person very politely, a man sometimes doubt about her intention, and in the worst case, he doubts about her character even. Though, we claim to be from a civilized society, why then, this irony exists in our society? The reasons may be many. One of the main reasons may be that, we are so habituated with dealing persons with bad behavior and ill-temperament, the moment we find someone good, we either, doubt his/her integrity/ courage etc. and behave him/her as a lesser mortal.'

'But, in office, it is more evident!' my friend contended.

'Yes, it may be. But, from my experience in office for the last 28 years, I learnt that, good behavior garners respect from 95% of the total employees, both seniors and juniors. Yes, I do agree, some rotten apples are there. You have to deal with them separately.' I tried to convince him.

'Yes, you may be right, we normally do not remember good things and good experiences, only bad experiences come to our mind again and again.' He admitted with a sigh.

'What is the matter my friend? I asked him sympathetically. He narrated the story given below:

His side of the story is given below:

My friend had been working in that particular office for the last few years. Though he was not the Head of the Division, he was heading a unit of thirty odd persons. Everybody knew, my friend was a very soft spoken person and he always used to maintain a cordial relation with his colleagues, both seniors and juniors. Everything was fine till the last year.

In the last year a group of five junior officers joined in the Division out of which two have joined in his unit. Out of these two officers one was very sincere in his work, therefore there was no problem with him. But the other one had some attitudinal problem towards office work. He never said no to any work, but he would make a point, not to do any work allotted to him. His immediate boss complained about the attitudinal problem of his subordinate quite regularly. But being a soft hearted man, my friend ignored and advised his junior to be more compassionate to him, as he was still very young.

But my friend's supportive actions embolden this new comer, so much so that, he started avoiding routine works and even ignored written orders. He started sending files to his immediate boss, as if he had given a written order to his boss or alternatively, he used to submit files as if, file was submitted by a very junior official. When this was reported by his junior officer, my friend got angry. He ordered to submit the file in a proper way. From the next day onwards, the newly joined officer took leave pretending (not sure) that, he was suffering from fever. My friend doubted that, this boy would join office only after his boss would submit the file of his own, as it was a time bound work.

'What about other three junior officers working other units?' I asked my friend.

'Except one, the other two had also some initial problems. However, they are positive towards their allotted works now and they are progressing quite satisfactorily now.

'Then, how can you say that, all juniors are trying to avoid works if his/her boss is compassionate! You have to deal that boy separately without any sympathy.' I concluded.

I could not be able to know whether my friend agreed to my suggestion or not, but so far I am concerned, I understand there is no thumb rule to treat all juniors alike. As all bosses are not same, all juniors also cannot be painted with the same brush. Man management itself is a huge task in modern day business.

Chapter: 51

Forgiving Enemies

I am told by many persons many a times that I should forgive my enemies. In reality, it is a real tough proposition to forgive your enemies. I also know, that is good for me, even though I tried many a times but, I failed to do so because it really need very strong will power to do so.

But a few days back, a thought struck me. Do my enemies actually harm me or not? Or harm has been done by somebody else?

Yes, I feel sometimes, friends and relatives are more harmful than my enemies because, sometimes they are more demanding than necessary. Sometimes, meeting them itself made you exhausted, but still they may not be satisfied. This affects your health-both mentally and physically. But these are necessary evils in our life. This problem is not only for me; even I may be a problem for others.

Who are our enemies? We see some of them (human and animals) and some of them, we cannot see through our naked eyes (virus, bacteria, worms inside our bodies etc). But your more harmful enemies are living inside you; in your mind. They are like worms in your stomach, they live on your blood; they suck your blood day and night, but you cannot get rid of them permanently. When you take de-worming medicine, they will lie low for few months and again they will raise their heads and start sucking your blood gleefully. But seldom have we counted these enemies, rather conveniently we choose to forget them.

What are those enemies? Our desire to have those things for which, we may not be deserving and lusts for someone who are not supposed to be ours. These are more harmful enemies than those seen by others or at least detected by medical tests. Desire for better life is not wrong-but desire to have someone else's property or someone else spouse is dangerous and sometimes may be fatal. There is an old saying, 'Lust leads to sins and sins lead to death.

Finally, since I cannot control the enemies residing in my mind totally, I do not have any moral right to hate my outside enemies, particularly those human enemies, who did actually very little harm to me. This is my latest (no, not the last one) realization towards the enemies who are roaming outside gleefully with a satisfaction that they had harmed me and I could not take any revenge on them.

Chapter: 52

Secular India

A friend of mine from a country which was a part of USSR asked me during the recess of an international conference (2013), 'Are you a Muslim?'

'No, I am a Hindu.' I replied.

'But Muslims must be the majority in your country!'

'Sorry, again, I have to say, no. Hindu is the religion of majority of the people in India. There are more than thousand small and big religious groups in India, out of which we consider for tabulation purposes six major religious groups.' I tried to explain.

'But, I have noticed, all the major roads in New Delhi are named after Muslim rulers, like Akbar, Humayun, Shahjehan, Sher Shah etc.' She was not convinced.

'That is the beauty of India! India is the largest democracy in the world. Our Prime Minister is a Sikh (at that time Dr. Manmohan Singh was the Prime Minister of India) with hardly 2% of the total population. The Chairman of the ruling coalition, Ms. Sonia Gandhi is a born catholic, which also comprises about another 2% of the total population. Our Defence Minister, Mr. Anthony is also a catholic and the Minister of External Affairs, Md.

Salman Khursid is a Muslim. The Chief of the Army, General Vikram Singh is also a Sikh, while the majority of the population are Hindus.' I concluded.

She was surprised and concluded, 'I salute your country's secular credentials and democratic values. I would prefer to be born in India next time, if I get a second chance!'

I could very well find her genuineness in her voice. Once again I realized, East or West, Indian subcontinent (Baring one or two rogue countries) is the best.

Chapter: 53

Pain of Publishing Books

An Assamese friend of mine 2001 asked me a very interesting question, 'I am going to publish a (in Assamese) story book. As a statistician, you tell me, how many copies, I have to print?'

I told him, 'Ok, let me calculate. There are about one crore Assamese people, out of which about 50 lakh know reading and writing. Out of that 50 lakh people, 47 lakh will never read books. Out of those three lakh, about 50 thousand may have the habits of reading books after purchasing (rest of the people will read after borrowing only). Out of these 50 thousand people, how many of them know you personally?'

He was already very much disappointed, and murmured, 'May be two thousand.'

'Ok then, you make prints of only five hundred copies of your book. With little efforts, you will be able to sell 200 copies and rest of the copies you distribute free of cost among your friends!'

He did not take my advice and printed five thousand copies.

After five years, when I was on an official tour to Guwahati, I met my friend and asked about the book. He said, 'Your estimate was wrong!'

'That is great! All books were sold?' I exclaimed.

'Yes, Out of five thousand copies, I sold 157 copies with great difficulty, around two hundred copies were given as complimentary by keeping my books at their residences/tables forcefully. Some of them were even returned. And finally, last year I sold all copies to a vendor @Rs.5/- a kilo. Therefore, I was able to sell all 5000 copies of book, as against your expectation of just to be able to sell only 500 copies.' He told with a laugh.

'The amount my wife got from the sell, had kept at the pedestal of idol of Lakshmi with a prayer that I should not venture again to write anything which reduces my friend circle.' He concluded with a sigh.

I did not have any word to console my friend at that time. Though now, I have a few words of consolation for my friend, I do not want to tell those words in public.

Chapter: 54

Bush Pig

Sometimes we do not have a proper answer to a simple and straight forward question. During an official visit to a place (I do not want to mention the name of the city), I came across such a question. One of my very close acquaintances asked me, "Am I that bad, that my subordinate nicknamed me as a 'bush pig'?"

Instead of answering the question, I asked him, "How do you know that?"

"A few days back an apprentice told me this when I scolded him for not passing an official message to a lady officer who happened to be (apparently) very polite to me. He told me that, he actually passed on the message, but subsequently the lady was telling a lie and blaming the apprentice for not acting upon the message.

When I told him that, she is a very good and obedient officer, how he could blame her for his own fault, he mischievously smiled and told me that I might have a wrong impression about the lady. I was intrigued by his mischievous smile and asked him why he is saying so.

On this he told me, 'Sir, Madam always refer you as a bush pig.'

I became very angry and warned him that he might lose his job for making such false allegation against a good officer, that too a lady.

But, this time, he answered again with lot of confidence in his voice, 'I am not telling a lie, sir. Even sir, your phone number is also saved in her mobile phone as 'bush pig'.

This time I lost temper and shouted, 'Get out of my room and do not show your face.'

But after some time, I got back my wits and called the lady to my room and with a friendly manner asked her mobile pretending that, I might be buying mobile phone of similar model. She hesitantly handed over her mobile and wasting no time I made a call from my mobile. To my shock, 'bush pig' had been flashed. I did not tell her anything.

But after few days I came to know that, she is planning to complain against me to my seniors 'for my misbehavior to a lady.' I do not know whether, she will lodge a complaint or not, but I am totally disturbed."

I too do not have an answer.

Neither I can confirm nor otherwise, his side of the story!

But to pacify him, I told him, 'This may be a 'one off case'. Further, I call my youngest daughter by many names, some are funny and some may be objectionable to an unknown person. But we have an understanding; we love each other very much. The lady may also have lot of respect for you, but--. Again in our college days, we used to call somebody as 'petu (fatty)' or 'lambu (lanky), it does not mean that we do not love them nor we do not have any respect for them.' I tried to justify the action of the lady officer.

Perhaps, he was not convinced!

Chapter: 55

Kiss of Death

'I may die in the next few minutes or so.' Probably few may have this experience once in a life time and very few may have this experience more than once. Thankfully, I am coming in the list of 'very few' who has experienced the experience more than once.

However, I want to share one of those experiences which was experienced by me few years back.

In January, 2013, I boarded a flight from Vienna to Delhi on time. But after we got into the aircraft, we were told that take off might be little late due to overloading of cargo. I was thrilled with a sadistic pleasure, 'Oh! Austrian airlines are also at par with our very own beloved Air India for being late!'

Finally, when we started, it was neat two hours' late.

In the meantime, a young person sitting next to me introduced himself. He used to utter 'Sir' word in every sentence and being a man of 50+, I understood that he would submit a request which normally no co-passenger would like to agree to oblige.

Normally, I used to reach airport well in advance and I ask for an aisle seat and usually I get it. That time also I got the desired seat and this gentleman was sitting beside me. After few minutes he told, 'I have a request to make you, sir!'

'Go ahead, probably, your wife is sitting on a middle row seat and none is ready to exchange it. Now you have found me apparently very friendly to you and that is why, you want to submit your unsolicited request. Is not it?'

With little hesitation, he said, 'Yes sir.'

'Why you did not come little early?' I asked him sarcastically. He kept mum. At least, I was happy that, he had not blamed his wife.

'Ok, show me your seat and call your wife.' He was surprised to hear my words and thanked profusely even before, he called his wife. After looking at his wife, I understood his anxiety for not getting a seat for her besides his own. She was a very beautiful lady in her early thirties. The lady politely thanked me for exchanging my seat with her. I told him that I was not going to shift my hand bag and asked him to show my seat. He escorted me to his seat which was at the middle row having five seats and the seat was exactly at the middle. I am sure none in this world will prefer that seat.

With customary, 'Excuse me' to my fellow passengers, I occupied my new seat. On my left, I found a smelly (smelling with gin or vodka) gentleman but on the right side I found the right person, a forty plus cute and slim Indian lady.

After settled down on my seat, I asked the lady, 'Are you an Indian?' just for a confirmation. With American ascent, she told me, 'Yes, but an American citizen.'

'I am sure, you are not a businessman. Where are you working?' With a beautiful smile she asked me.

'I am a Government of India's Babu.' With a grin I told her. 'But how do you assume that I am not a businessman?'

'Otherwise you would not have changed your aisle seat with a cramped seat!'

After that, ice was broken with that lady and I found her one of the best co-passengers in my life. She happened to be a daughter of a famous physician of India, married to a professor of a listed University of USA, mother of two teenage girls.

We had discussions on different topics ranging from education to politics; corruption to honesty, mythology to history and probably no topics was untouched. We were so engrossed in our discussion; seven and half hours of our journey appeared to be only half an hour journey. For the first time, I did not take any drinks on board of an International flight.

We reached the sky of Delhi and about to land at Indira Gandhi International Airport at around 8 O' clock in the evening and at that time the dreaded announcement was made by the pilot, 'This is your Captain --, I have to make an important announcement. Before our departure from Vienna, we had informed you that, the delay was due to overloading of cargo. But that was not true- actually we had problems with one of our wings and same was repaired. Most unfortunately, now again on the way, it became defunct. But do not worry. Now, I hope we shall land the craft safely with the grace of God and my 20 years' experience along with the help of my other crew members. Pray to God for a safe landing.'

After the announcement a gloom had descended in the aircraft. Even the sound of the respiration of the fellow passengers became loud enough to create a fear in others' mind.

What came to my mind after hearing the announcement? I travelled more than hundred times by air but, every time I travel by air, I used to have some awkward feelings which use to come to my mind, if the aircraft is going to have a crash landing/ an accident etc. But I always pray to the Almighty, if I have to die in a plane accident, so be it; but my only wish is that, the accident should take place near to an airport, so that my dead body can be retrieved and identified!

After the announcement, I had a mixed reaction: hopefully the pilot would be able to make a safe landing and if he failed, it would be an accident near to the airport that too in my city of residence. It would mean that my wish (best among the worst situations) would be fulfilled by God.

Anyway, we passed our few moments without breathing (probably) and then we heard that beautiful sound 'a moderate thud' and with little vibration after which the aircraft steadied itself. A burst of clapping sound submerged the whining sound of the aircraft. Many hugged their near and dear ones. I did not hug anybody nor clap and only asked my co-passenger, 'Why all have clapped?'

She, with her big eyes, with astonishment asked, 'Have you not heard the announcement?'

'Nope' I said.

'You are really incorrigible!' She gave me a beautiful smile.

Did she hug me before we departed? I would have liked to do that. But she did not initiate a hug and I did not dare to initiate.

She is still my friend and probably, she is the best co-passenger I have ever traveled with, till date!

I cannot finish my story without thanking the businessman and his lovely wife, with whom I had to exchange my seat reluctantly!

Chapter: 56

Liking for Elder's Dresses

The incident happened few decades back.

I was tense, as my boss was visiting my regional office for the first time, which I was heading. It was a cold day of December, at Kohima. I had to go to Dimapur which is 74 KM away from Kohima and the only airport of Nagaland, to receive my boss. I was in a hurry, as I have to take a taxi from Kohima to Dimapur and I would have to indulge a tug of war with the taxi driver for fare, which had been exorbitant in Nagaland in those days.

When I came out of bath room, I saw my daughter, two year old, was wearing (?) my coat. My neatly ironed coat was in a mess with cerelac and some other liquid, might be dal already on many places over the coat. My shirt and pant were also not unscathed with eatables of my daughter.

You can understand my state of mind. Neither, I could scold her nor I was able to tell anything to my wife, who had recently delivered a baby boy. I was looking at her with despair on my eyes, but she was so engrossed with the neck tie to be worn by her, she did not notice even my presence. I took her in my arms and put her on the other end of the bed, and put on my dress. With my best efforts also I could not erase the stains on the coat. Having only one coat in my closet, I did not have any alternative, but to wear it and run to the taxi stand to hire a taxi to go to the airport.

At Dimapur airport, I met my boss, who was about fifty year old, asked me, 'Your toddler is a son or daughter?'

'She is daughter, two year old."

'She not only loves you, but your dresses also.'

His comments embarrassed me.

Seeing me embarrassed, he commented, 'Do not be embarrassed. These are the most beautiful moments of your life. Enjoy these moments, when, she will be a young lady, remembering these moments, you will cherish your life and these revered moments will be the most precious memory for you. When you will be of my age, these moments will matter more and you will only think why these moments are not coming back again. But it won't come back! You are lucky to have a daughter, a son will not wear your coats after attaining a certain age, but a daughter likes to wear her father's/ elder brother's coat even after marriage. Today, she spoiled your coat, but after some years, she will see that your coat is spotless, whenever, you are going for an important assignment.'

Things are unfolding as the senior predicted. My son used to wear my coat till few years back and stopped wearing my dress. He developed his own dress sense which may not be similar to that of mine. Sometimes he forced his dress sense on me, though I admire his dress sense, I seldom acknowledge in front of him.

On the other hand, both the daughters use to wear my coat occasionally even now and stand before a mirror. At the very tender age, they smiled and sometimes danced and sometimes giggled. They put my caps on their small heads and put their fingers and use to gauge, how much space remains to fill up to fit the cap. I do not know, what they see in the mirror by wearing my dress, but still I love it. It reminds me when they spoiled my dress and giggled without any remorse and still I could not scold, but hugged and kissed them!

It also reminds me of my sisters who used to wear my coat/blazer without my permission which ensued a big fight. When I was young, I used to fight with my sister, but once I crossed teen age, I stopped fighting for wearing my dress. Probably I have mellowed down further when my daughter used to wear my dress. I do not know what will be my reaction, when my granddaughter wear my dress and spoil it thoroughly!

Chapter: 57

Birthday Wish

What best gift can a father give to his daughter on her birth day? Anything may be less than her expectation! Normally every father faces this problem, unless she tells her father beforehand what gift she wants. So trying to give a surprise gift, may be dampener for both of them.

I also find it difficult every time when birth day comes for my two daughters. However, recently I found more difficulty when I had to give a birth day gift to one of my spiritual daughters. Though it appears to be simple, I find it very difficult to choose amongst variety of gift items flooded in the market. After a long thought, I came to the conclusion that I can give a gift which is nothing but an assurance to my daughter (spiritual) coming from my heart. I jotted down a letter which is reproduced here:

'My dear child,

At the very outset, on your birth day, I convey my best wishes for your success in all spheres of life in the coming days and hope you will emit more lights on your next birth day. After breaking my head, what gift will be suitable on this beautiful occasion, I come to a conclusion that I am going to give a gift which is not marketable, which is invaluable and priceless. What can be that? An assurance! Yes it is nothing but an assurance; hopefully no father has given to his daughter (spiritual) on her birth day.

However, I assure you, in the process, I do not want to try to take any place equivalent to your father who happened to be the best person in the world for you. But I definitely want to occupy the distant second position who may think always best for you.

I have given you permission by which, you may approach me at any time, at any place and in any circumstances for any assistance whenever you would feel the need for that. I know, I have limitations, as every human being has, I may be found to be useless to help you out, but I assure you that, I shall try my best to help you out- but I wish that day should never come. I know, my brave daughter can solve all her problems at her level singlehandedly. But still, I promise you to standby, if necessary, like a solid rock at your back, for your decisions, may be wrong or right, as I do for other daughters.

I love you, my dear child, not as much as your Dad loves you. But still I can contest with anybody for the second position till your marriage; those love you as his own daughter.

Be brave, my dear one, I am, shall be with you.'

I did not know how she took my assurances. But I became a relieved man after writing the letter.

Chapter: 58

Birthday Wishes to a Junior

In a similar situation, I was caught in indecisiveness, what best gift I can give on birth day of a junior! After a long thought, I came to a conclusion that, I can give a gift which is nothing but an assurance like what I have given to my spiritual daughter which has been reproduced in the earlier chapter. However, I would have also relished, had I got such an assurance from any of my bosses:

'Dear bro/sis,

It is customary to give a gift on one's birth day. But instead of giving a traditional gift, I am giving you something different.

I know that you have high regards for your earlier boss, who happened to be a dream boss, for anyone likes to have. Fortunately, I also worked under her for a pretty long time. Whatever I learnt during her tenure, probably, I have not learnt throughout my service life. I am talking about good things only. Occasionally, whenever, she scolds me, I had full confidence that, it would help me in building my future/career. He/she taught me like a subject teacher in a higher secondary. Therefore, even in wildest dream, I do not want to (even try to) take any place equivalent to my previous boss who happened to be the best boss both of us ever had. She was the best for all of us.

But I shall put my hat in the ring to be the second best boss for you. For that, what I should do? I thought for a day and come to a conclusion that, I should assure you something which I can fulfill with little or no difficulty at all. My assurance is jotted down below for your records:

You can approach me at any time, at any place and in any circumstances for any assistance whenever you would feel the need, whether official or personal. I shall try my best to help you out- but I wish that day should never come. I know, as a junior to me in age and official capacity, you can solve all your problems at your level singlehandedly. But still, I promise to standby, if necessary, like a solid rock at your back, even you have not taken any written approval on file. I promise you, not to put you before the enemy lines, no matter, even though, I may scold you right and left, when we discuss the matter in house. You never have to worry about your annual appraisal, no matter how many times you argue with me, so long, we have a common goal to serve our country better.

I love you, my dear friend, not as much as your family loves you. But still, I can contest with anybody who may be your best well-wishers, other than your family members.

Be brave and honest, my dear friend, I am, shall be with you, so long we try to serve our country in a better way.'

After sending this letter to my junior, I was pondering how many boss of mine stood behind me like a rock during my thick and thin days. I am very happy that, I found some. However, during course of service, I found, some are just opposite what I have written in my assurance letter to my junior. But in the hind sight, I thought, I should be thankful to those also, as they gave me the opportunity to become a rock behind the boss who placed a barrier of wax before the barrage of gunshots (not literally) from the enemies.

Chapter: 59

Relation

Kanak has two daughters; both are settled and live in two different cities of south India. Kanak loves both the daughters equally, but after, the younger also left home in 2012, he was emotionally devastated. After his mother's death, he used to call his younger daughter as Rimi-ma, adding ma after her name.

For few days, after her placement at Bangalore, he could neither sleep properly nor eat properly. Whenever he used to for his meal, he remembered, how his younger daughter used to scold him for taking more fried things on his plate than he supposed to take. He equally missed the elder daughter, Nimi, who is more sober in her talks, who is now living in Chennai, never scolded him for eating more or for doing something nonsense. She simply correct those things without uttering a single word. Her love for Kanak was more underlying than explicit. But when she left for her job, at least the younger one was with them to fill up the gaps of the elder daughter. Scientists say, this syndrome of voidness after children leave their parental house is called ENS (Empty Nest Syndrome). It appears, Kanak was also suffering from this syndrome.

During this period a young girl, Nisha had joined Kanak's office as a direct recruit officer. Her age is in between of his daughters' age. She is three year younger than his elder daughter and one year older than his younger daughter.

This young girl had to report Kanak directly for one month as her immediate boss was on leave. After initial hesitations for few days, she started opening up and Kanak noticed that her style of talking and body language is similar to that of his younger daughter. She is from a middle class family of Delhi and is living with her parent along with her younger brother, studying in an Engineering college.

After one month, her boss joined and naturally interaction with the girl reduced considerably. But in the meantime, both Kanak and Nisha developed a close bonding. Nisha started coming to his chamber at least once in a day to say 'hello' to him. Kanak started waiting for those ten /twenty minutes of their togetherness. He realized that this girl was filling the emptiness of his daughters up to some extent.

After six months he realized that this girl was behaving exactly like his younger daughter and used to scold him right and left whenever he did not take medicine or meal in time or took many cups of tea. He started to like her scolding and intentionally did not follow her dictates, so that she could scold as if she was his own daughter.

Despite of her closeness to Kanak, she never allowed any interference in their official relations with personal relations and vice-versa. She was very fast in learning the official works and became an officer of repute within a very short span of time.

Days passed and relation between Kanak and Nisa also grew very fast and ten minutes conversation extended to one hour and slowly Nisa's visit to Kanak's room was not limited to one visit only. Slowly their relation extended to both the families as well. Nisha and Rimi became good friends and she came to know all behavioral activities which Rimi passed on. Kanak's elder daughter, as usual, was not very much in the loop. Kanak started taking Nisha along with him for attending all the official engagement for his official assistance. This became an eyesore to many similarly placed officers. But that did not deter, Kanak to change his position, as Nisha was also comfortable to such an arrangement.

A few years ago, Kanak had to deliver a lecture at an institution located at Mumbai. On the same day Nisha had also another official engagement at Mumbai. Therefore, both have decided to go to Mumbai by the same flight and return on the same day by an evening flight. But thanks to the airlines, the evening flight was cancelled on unavoidable circumstances and those passengers having return tickets were lodged in a hotel very near to the airport. As Kanak and Nisha had a common ticket they were allotted a single room. Kanak protested to it but Nisha agreed to the proposal gleefully.

Having no alternative, he followed Nisha to the room. The room was quite spacious with a king-size bed and a three seated sofa set. After reaching the room, Kanak told Nisha that she could sleep on the bed and he would occupy the sofa.

Nisha shot back, 'If Rimi is with you today, will you not sleep on the same bed, then why cannot you sleep with me. Ok, if you are not sleeping with me, I shall sleep on the sofa.'

Saying this she entered to the bath room. Kanak sat on the sofa for a while and he waited for Nisha's return from the bathroom. After few minutes when Nisha came out, Kanak told Nisha, 'OK, both of us will sleep on the bed. But do not blame me afterwards as I am a notorious snorer.' After telling this Kanak went to the bath room.

After ten minutes, when he came to the room, Kanak saw Nisha was in deep sleep and occasionally snoring also. Putting the dim light on, at the far end of the bed, he lied. He was worried to go to sleep, thinking if during his sleep his body touched Nisha, she might think otherwise.

But when sleep caught him he did not know, till the doorbell rang. He tried to get up, but he could not do that because both the legs of Nisha were comfortably placed on his belly, exactly similar fashion as Rimi used to do while sleeping with him. She also made a perpendicular position with Kanak as Rimi used to do. For a moment, Kanak felt that actually Rimi was sleeping with him. Without disturbing her sleep, he removed her legs and went to attend the doorbell.

Hotel attendant told Kanak to be ready as the bus to the airport will leave within twenty minutes. Kanak went to the bath room and after coming from the bath room, he tried to awake Nisha. But she was still in fast sleep.

Kanak, at first called her to get up, but there is no sign of getting up from Nisha's side. Then, Kanak put his hand on Nisha's shoulder and asked her, 'Nisha-ma, get up, otherwise we shall miss the bus.'

Nisha still in sleep and said, 'Papa, let me sleep for another five minutes.'

It appeared she was under the impression that she was sleeping in her own residence. This time Kanak raised his voice and put both hands on her shoulders and said, 'Nishama, get up.'

This time she got up and said, 'Oh sorry sir. What happened?'

On the airport, Nisha asked Kanak, 'Sir, did I disturb you in your sleeping? I am sorry sir, during my sleep, I have a habit of rotating on my bed.'

'Yes, you did. You gave me a real daughter, in the last night. From today, you may call me as Papa, of course not in the office.'

'May I also call you 'W' (Rimi calls Kanak 'W'' fondly sometimes to extract more love and attentions)'?

Nisha smiled sheepishly.

Chapter: 60

Fenny-The Epitome of Beauty

It is a real story of a girl who can wither turbulence in all weather. I changed the name of the girl and situation to protect the privacy of the girl. She is one of the greatest heroes of my life. I deliberately use the word 'hero', instead of the word 'heroine'.

I am sure, you have also met many 'Fennys' in your daily life. In most of the cases we may not have sufficient time or inclination to hear the real stories of those 'Fennys'. I am trying to submit my solemn tribute to all the 'Fennys' who are mostly un-noticed by most of us while performing our routine duties. We seldom realize every smiling face may have a turbulent present or turbulent past or both. Hope my readers will appreciate the real story of a girl, who might be akin to another girl known to them and living in their vicinities.

'Why you are keeping cropped hair like a soldier?' I asked the young lady of 28 with a mischievous tone.

'Oh, uncle, don't you know, I am a soldier?' With a beautiful smile she replied to my teasing question.

'Then, what you are doing here?'

'I also do not know why I am here?' With another beautiful smile she replied.

‘Anyway, how is the food? Are you enjoying?’ She asked me this time professionally.

‘Yeah, food is nice. I am thoroughly enjoying. But again I am asking the same question, how and why you are here? Are you a management student?’ I stuck to my earlier question while relishing my food.

‘No uncle, I am not a management student. Basically I am an engineer, passed out from a college of Bihar. In my college, there was practically no teacher to teach us and therefore there was no class to attend by all the students including me. Though the college had very impressive buildings and other infrastructural facilities, no teacher wanted to stay in the college for more than a month. We had a merry time for all the four years in my college. I do not know how the management was able to arrange engineering degree certificates for all of us. But without iota of knowledge of engineering how can I get a job of an engineer? May be due to my whitish complexion and Aryan eyes, the hotel owner gave me this job so that I can attract few young customers of the city.’ She again smiled.

‘Why you blamed the youngsters only? Even old people like me, may come again and again to your restaurant to see your beautiful smile.’ With a broad smile, I remarked with another teasing tone.

‘Thank you uncle. At least you appreciate my smile. But my father told me on my face, at least hundred times, that my smile irritates him.’ For the first time she looked little bit upset.

But immediately she composed herself and with a beautiful smile she again said, ‘It may be due to Hindi proverb, gharka murgi daal barabar (chicken curry made of home grown chicks tastes same as the taste of normal pulses).'

'I have also two daughters. I always like their smiles and pray to God, they should be able to smile always in their lives.' I objected as I could not agree to her statement.

'Because you must have only one wife and both the daughters are borne from the same wife.' She said without showing any emotion.

'Oh, I see. You are from the first wife of your father and therefore, he utters those words to satisfy the ego of your stepmother.' This time, with a sympathetic tone, I commented.

'Yes Uncle, after divorce, both have married, so I have both stepfather and stepmother at different places.'

We kept mum for some time.

Her name was Fenny. Her mother was from Arunachal, a province from North Eastern part of India and father was from Kerala, a South Indian province of India. She was a very beautiful girl with short hair and long attractive legs flaunted thorough her shorts. She must be more than five feet seven inches. She looked extremely beautiful for her straight body posture with beautiful curves on her slim body. Her teeth were as white as white marble. Her skin was as smooth as a billiard board. Her smile was contagious. Nail-polished fingers were too attractive to remove eyes for few seconds by anyone who had a look on those. In one word, she was as beautiful as an imaginary goddess of beauty. Any young man was likely to be attracted to her by her husky voice. Even at my age, I preferred to talk to her though there were at least another six ladies and six boys to cater my needs as I visited the restaurant much before it was flooded with the regular guests. I had to visit the restaurant at around 11 O'clock as I had to proceed to another town, Ziro by road after taking a brunch (breakfast cum lunch).

The restaurant was located at the periphery of Naharlagaun, the largest city, of Arunachal Pradesh. Though I normally stay at Itanagar, capital town of Arunachal Pradesh and sixteen KM from Naharlagun, in all my official visits, I always prefer to take breakfast, lunch and dinner in that particular restaurant because of variety of international cuisines served by them.

As I was taking my brunch, I started my conversation with the beautiful lady, who also showed interest in talking with me. After few minutes of our conversation, she sat in front of me after taking a formal permission from me. Normally, hotel boys and girls do not sit in front of any customer while serving food.

Fenny had a turbulent childhood as her parents decided to divorce when she was hardly four and finally divorced on her fifth birthday. She was able to recall the fighting and shouting of her parents on trivial issues even after many years passed since then. The fights were basically coming out from the basic cultural differences of the two communities representing by her parents. Her mother was a Christian tribal lady and her father was a Hindu, Keralite. Both were different almost in all respects, from food habit to religion, costumes to family values. Climatic condition of the two provinces were also complete different, Arunachal Pradesh's climate is akin to

European climate and Kerala's climate is that of African climate.

Her father fell in love with her mother when he was posted at Arunachal Pradesh. They had a beautiful married life for one year and in the meantime they were blessed with Fenny. Six months after Fenny's birth, her father got a job in his home state. Then he moved along with his family to his home state. Then onwards, their conflict had started and culminated in a divorce. One year after, Fenny's father got married to another lady from his own caste from his home state. Her mother also followed the suit after two years of their divorce.

However, there was only one silver lining in Fenny's life, Fenny's father took full responsibility of her education and to be honest, she remained grateful to her father for giving sufficient money for her education till her graduation. And might be due to that financial reason, her mother also did not object to her ex-husband to bring her up as a Hindu till Fenny had completed her education.

However, a few years ago when she had visited her step father's place, with some emotional black mailing by her mother, Fenny was converted to a Christian. Therefore, when I met her Fenny was a devout Christian as per her own statement.

Again following her parents footsteps, she fell in love with a Muslim young man from Lucknow with whom she planed her marriage after one year. At that time, he was working in Dubai and she dreamt for a beautiful married life with him in Dubai. However, the memory of a failed marriage of her parents used to give sufficient worries for her future married life.

'Both my parents love me very much. Both of them want, I should be with them during my vacation.' She concluded with a statement which, I thought, was full of sarcastic venom.

'That is good. At least they still love you very much.' I said the sentence without attaching any genuineness in my voice. She is intelligent enough to understand my tone.

Laughing loudly, she said, 'Uncle you are very clever. You understood, what the ground reality is.'

'Is not their behaviour out of true love for you?' I wanted to know the truth from her mouth.

'They want to prove before others that I am loved by their family more than their counterparts. They do not have iota of love for me.' Instead of weeping, she smiled again.

'That is not true my child. Definitely they love you. But both of them dare not to show their love for you in front of their present spouses and your younger step-siblings expecting some strong reprisals.' I tried to console the young lady.

Though from her facial expression, it was clear that she was not convinced, she did not discuss on the issue any further.

Naturally, she became unhappy day by day as she grew older after divorce of her parents. She was put to a boarding school by her father once her mother was married to her stepfather. Her frustrations goes in the Northern direction as the couples were blessed with her step-siblings after their respective marriages. Slowly, in the emotional world, for both the parents, Fenny became a non-entity. As I have not met her parents, I cannot say whether, she became actually a non-entity or not, but at least she thinks like that.

Despite of growing feeling of neglect, so long she was a student it was tolerable for her. Once she became an unemployed youth in her early twenties, her frustration became unbearable for her. Slowly, but steadily she became a victim of depression.

Two years back she had to be hospitalized for a case of acute depression. She was put under heavy medication. After taking treatment from a group of dedicated doctors in Channai and a series of motivational speeches by some Christian clergies, she realized, life was beyond love from parents. She understood, all human beings are selfish and her parents are also not different from others. When they remarried they only thought for their comfort and emotional support. They probably never thought what a turmoil had to be faced by their little daughter when both of them decided to go for remarriage. She was told by those motivational clergies to love herself and to become little bit selfish. She took almost a year to come out her depression. Once she came out of her depression, she never looked back. For her, that part of her life was a closed chapter for her forever.

In the meantime, she met her lover at the Chennai airport while coming from Chennai to Guwahati dramatically when her flight was cancelled by the airlines without any prior information. As she was worried where to stay for the night all alone, a young man told her that she should not be worried for the overnight stay at Chennai as he was with his mother and sister and she could share a hotel room with his mother and sister. That small gesture from the unknown young man blossomed into a full blown love affairs in due course of time.

She started dreaming for a better future with him for the rest of her life.

At that time, she was free from all medication of depression.

'Now I am free from all family bonding. During my vacation or leave, I use to visit different parts of India. If I can earn more money, I shall take some tour to some foreign countries as well. As of now I do not have sufficient money.' She smiled apologetically.

"What about your honeymoon plan?' I wanted to see another smile on her face.

'I do not know exactly where we can go for our honeymoon. However, I know I have to fight another battle before my marriage also. My father wants, I should marry a Hindu Keralite boy. He thinks a boy from their community will be the best husband in the world for me. Diametrically opposite views are ushered by my mother. According to her, Keralite Hindu boys from my father's community will be the worst possible husband for me. Her sample size, though limited to her husband's family only, her opinion is as strong as a Himalayan rock. She wants my husband should be an Arunachali and from her own tribe. I do not know, how they will react when I shall tell them that I am going to marry a Muslim boy from Lucknow working in Dubai.' This time she gave me a faint smile different from her earlier free flow smiles.

'But I always think about crossing the bridge only after reaching the edge of the bridge. Till then, I want to chill.'

This time again, her natural smile emerged from her face.

'How, the family of the young man reacted when they first came to know about your love affairs?'

'They welcomed the affair.' This time she smiled with a sense of happiness.

I wanted to change the topic of her unhappy childhood and her conflict of mind during her young age. At that time, I did not want to discuss also about the pros and cons of three religions. Neither had I wanted to discuss about the possibility of reservations of her parents to her marriage to a Muslim youth. Life of the lovely girl Fenny, was already in turmoil. Therefore, I asked the question which is the first line of my story of the brave girl to lighten up for our discussion. But something else was in store for me which I never thought in my wildest dream to hear from the young lady.

I asked the young beautiful lady of late twenties with a mischievous tone, why she was keeping cropped hair like a soldier, while sipping my hot and sour soup served by the young lady in her restaurant.

After having some humorous conversations on her short hair as mentioned earlier, she said with a beautiful smile, 'Uncle, I have a disease. Due to the disease, after taking a specific medicine, I use to lose my long hair. Keeping my hair short, I am able to maintain the beauty of my hair.'

'What is the disease? Have you not consulted a good doctor?' With a serious voice I asked the young lady.

'Yeah, I am consulting the best oncologists of Tata Memorial Hospital, Mumbai. They say, my white blood cells are blooming like white tulips in the spring. They are trying to control the white tulips with some medicines. They had told me on my last visit two months ago, if they would not be able to control the over-blooming of the white tulips in the next six months, they will have no option but to go for an operation to evict the roots of the tulips. But the problem is, new roots have to be implanted by borrowing some roots from the gardens of one of my siblings. Siblings from the same parents are reluctant to donate few roots from their gardens. Therefore, I am not expecting any of my step-siblings will be ready to lend some of their roots to plant in my garden.' She smiled again.

I could not dare to ask any more questions to the smiling girl.

I was wondering how a cancer patient, taking chemotherapy on regular intervals, can describe her disease as an analogy of blooming tulips in the spring. Unfortunately, I even did not know, in which season, tulips bloom. I could not understand, how she could describe so eloquently, bone-marrow transplantation as transplanting of few roots of tulips in a flower garden.

'If she does not get a donor for bone marrow transplantation–' I could not think beyond that. An unknown shivering sense passed through my spine. I was virtually frozen to a piece of ice.

She, with a smile again started. 'Uncle, I can assure you one thing for sure, I shall not surrender to the disease meekly without a fight irrespective of getting some roots from my siblings' garden or not. I will also not care, whether my parents give me their helping hands to me or not in my fight against the disease. Even if, I am losing the battle, you will see me always smiling whenever you meet me in the near future.'

On seeing mum she again told me, 'Come to our restaurant again, uncle. Even though during your next visit I may have to travel to Mumbai to see the serious looking doctors, I shall tell my friends to take care of you nicely. Now a days, when none has time to peep into the daily events even of a friend, you are gracious enough to give me a patient hearing for more than an hour on our very first meeting. For that, I shall remain grateful to you.'

I did not have any answer to her genuine praise for me. Though, I knew that I did not deserve those praising words of her, I could not utter a single word. I could not say that, the fact of the matter, I always like to spend some quality time with some smiling beautiful ladies. For the first time in my life, before a young lady, I felt myself like a Lilliput who was standing before a towering giant.

I was sitting on my chair for few minutes without a single word till my escorting officer told me, 'Let us go sir, otherwise we shall not be able to reach Ziro before dusk.'

When I looked back from my car to the door of the restaurant, I saw her waiving her right hand with a beautiful smile on her face.

I asked myself, 'Will God save her simile for another fifty odd years?'

On the very next moment I thought, 'I do not know, whether God will save her or not, but if she dies early, world will be poorer by a brave soul.'

Fenny will remain one of my ultimate heroes of my life, irrespective of the result of the battle she was fighting for the last one year.

I shall remain grateful to God for giving me an opportunity to interact for more than an hour with a girl having nerve of steel and beauty of the goddess, Venus.

(It is a true story with changed name. I could not meet the girl on my next visit to the restaurant as she went to Mumbai for her checkup. On the third visit also I could not meet her because she had already left all of us forever. RIP)

Chapter: 61

How to Get Rid of Frustration

When you are frustrated most? Everyone in one's life has to experience hundred times the brunt of frustration. How we can overcome the frustration? What is frustration? What are main types of frustration? In this small article, I am trying to share with my readers some real stories experienced by myself or by some of my friends in their daily life. If after reading this article one can reduce his/ her frustration level even up to a little extent, I shall feel to be blessed for my efforts.

'Have you ever faced this situation in life, when you visit the residence of your new boss or new super boss for the first time, his wife came out to greet you and you are shell-shocked to see that she happened to be your ex-girlfriend, whom you had dumped few years back?' Subhankar asked me with a gloomy face.

'No, most of the bosses of mine are from North India who married their respective wives as per the dictums of their parents. Those who are from south India, their wives are mostly their cousins. Before my marriage, I was never been to south India, so no chance of having a South Indian girlfriend. Similarly, as you know, though I tried my luck with many beautiful girls from Delhi, they never thought I was fit for them. In my life, I had two Assamese

Bosses when I worked in Staff Selection Commission. Fortunately, I met the wives of both the bosses for the first time in my life, after they became my boss. So, I had no opportunity to face that problem. Further, unfortunately all the girlfriends of mine got older husbands than I and they are having officially inferior jobs than mine. However, some of the husbands are much wealthier (why I do not want to say) than I and to my heart burn, some of my ex-girlfriends are still maintaining killing beauty. Therefore, my friend, fortunately, I have never faced that problem in my life so far. However, from your question, I am sure you are facing the problem.' I cleared my position.

'Yeah.' He heaved a sigh.

'Up to what extent she was your girlfriend? Why you had ditched her?' I asked him with some excitement in my voice.

'Up to kissing on the lips only. I ditched her as my heart was stolen by another beautiful lady, who is now my nagging wife.' Subhankar said with another sigh.

I understand Subhankar's problem. He thought his ex-girlfriend was not up to the mark for him. To his utter disappointment, she was chosen as life partner by his own super boss who was also younger than him by two years.

But I wanted know, how he had tackled the immediate shock of his life.

'She coolly invited me to her house and introduced her husband that I was like a brother to her when we were in college and my girlfriend, who is presently my wife, was her best friend. Her husband took little interest in her introduction and told me that he does not believe in personal relation in office work and also told his wife that so far official matters are concerned she should not advocate in favour of her brother. When I heard the 'brother' word in my girlfriend's mouth once and then in her husband's mouth, I felt like getting two slaps on my face.' He was really upset.

'I understand your problem. Please avoid to meet your ex-girlfriend in future- that is the only advice I can give you for now.' I told him thoughtfully.

'I also vowed not to go to her home in future. But my problem has been enhanced when my immediate boss came to know that wife of my super boss is known to me from my college days, he told me to help him out from the hawkish eyes of my super boss. Neither, I can refuse the request of my immediate boss nor the strict warning of my super boss nor I want to face my ex-girlfriend. Further my problem has been enhanced when my wife came to know that wife of my super boss is the dumped girlfriend of mine. Once my wife was happy to snatch me from her clutch, now she also feels that she is also a loser alongwith me. Nowadays, she even taunts me for not capable of choosing persons in my life.' He stopped there.

'I cannot advise you what to do and how to solve the problem. I can only show my deepest sympathy on the issue. By the way, how your boss came to know that your super boss's wife is known to you? And how your wife came to know about her presence?' I asked.

'In a family get-together, Navanita, my ex-girlfriend told everyone that I was like her own brother and my wife is a friend of her from college days. I felt like, she slapped me once again in public and my wife also enjoyed her introduction by endorsing what Navanita was saying. I felt, my wife was spraying some salt on my wounds. Now I am really a frustrated man.' He put his hands on his head.

I thanked God silently, for not having a boss or super boss who had married one of many girlfriends. After all probability of happening of an event increases as and when value of numerator increases.

Definitely my friend is a frustrated man and rightly so.

I am giving another example of frustration when a friend is committing mistakes after mistakes to get rid of a frustration. His mistakes only enhanced his frustration level and he developed a guilty feeling over the time.

This friend of mine loved a girl from upper caste and upper class. Though he was intelligent and having a good job, the family of the girl rejected his marriage proposal considering the caste factor and the economic background he had come from. He proposed the girl to elope with him. But the girl refused and he got frustrated to an unbearable level. During that period he vowed to himself, 'I shall f—hundred ladies from her caste.'

Did he do the right thing by vowing such an unholy promise? No, in his pursuit to full-fill his promise to himself, he did all sort of nonsense in his life making his family life a hell.

It is said, becoming second best in any competition is the most frustrating for any individual. The competition may not be limited only to the field of sports, literature, cultural activities or professional. It may be extended to personal life or personal achievements of your near and dear ones.

There may be hundreds of reasons to become a frustrated person. In one of my books, I explained how both the biological father and the legal father became frustrated when their son was selected for the best administrative job in the country. The biological father could not claim that the brilliant young man was his illegal son and therefore, he was frustrated. On the other hand, whenever, the legal father was congratulated for his son's success, he has to swallow the humiliation silently knowing fully well that his legal son is not his biological son and is nothing but a product of illicit relation of his wife with another intelligent and more attractive person. In other words, for him the brilliant young man was nothing but a proof of betrayal by his wife. Unfortunately, he cannot tell anyone about the painful infidelity of his wife. Therefore, he is a frustrated person who is suffering silently from inside.

All the cases cited above are extreme personal reasons of frustration. However, in day to day life we become frustrated due to some genuine reasons and due to some avoidable reasons.

There may be different kind of frustrations. However, the frustrations can be classified into two broad categories: long time frustration and short term acute frustration. Long-time frustrations may linger for months, years and even for the whole life.

Let us understand what I have categorized a lifelong frustration. An officer who scored one mark short out of 2100 marks for an elite service, may have a lifelong frustration and whenever he come across the person who elbowed him out by only one mark, he feels the pain. Even in Olympic and in any other world competition, a sportsperson has a chance to show his/her prowess to other sportspersons who defeated him/her in the last edition of the game. But for the officer concerned never got a second chance in the next 35 odd years. Thus he becomes a frustrated man, unless he opted to think out of box to open another door of opportunity. But how many of us can do that?

Now I am giving another example of frustration of a person whom I met 33 years ago.

When I was in probation, I had to visit an office down south. In those days, in that particular organization when posted at the field level, the officers of that rank were very powerful, as he was not only the controlling officer but also appointing authority of the junior level technical officers and disciplinary authority for most of the officers and officials working under him. I met this powerful officer when I visited that office long back. I found him as a nice gentle man for me (might be because of the fact that I was going to hold the same rank after completion of my probation), but was a terror in the eyes of his juniors. However, within a day or two, I noticed one of the junior officers was ignoring his boss even before other officers without any fear and respect in his eyes. This all powerful officer always tried to avoid this arrogant subordinate in public and in many occasions he had to oblige this arrogant subordinate's unjustified demands also.

After noticing this unusual behaviour of the two officers for each other, one day I asked another officer, why he was so arrogant and why the powerful boss had to sulk humiliation in public in the hands of that arrogant subordinate.

'So you have also observed the unusual behaviour of Mr. X and our boss towards each other! It was not like that even three years back. Mr. X was also like us, fearful of our boss. But due to a turn of event three years back, the only son of X joined as the boss of the son of our boss in the State Government after clearing State Civil Service. From that day onwards, our boss became a frustrated man and Mr. X is bullying our boss.'

'How many years your boss has to suffer his frustration? When he is retiring?' I asked.

'Two more years.' The officer replied with a satisfaction in his voice. I understood, the officer was also happy to see the agony of the frustrated boss.

These are two examples of long term frustration. Now let us take few examples of short term frustration.

You are in a hurry to reach your office as early as possible as your boss called for a meeting and your vehicle refuses to start. You abandon the vehicle, but you are not getting an auto or taxi. You are likely to be a frustrated man till an auto-rickshaw agrees to drop you at your office even after taking a hefty unjustified fare.

You are in a hurry to reach the tenth floor to attend a meeting to be chaired by your Minister and at every stop your lift is stopping and at every floor some people are entering and some are going out. You may be sweating for an impending danger.

Some mid-term frustrations are also part of our lives. Your application for GPF withdrawal fund is lying with the sanctioning authority's table and he is on a week's leave, your frustration level go up on daily basis till the file is cleared.

Non ending fighting of your wife and your mother on trivial issues may be a major frustration for any married male. This may be an example of long-term or medium term of frustration depending upon how long they live together.

I am avoiding to tell you about bed room frustrations and frustrations of non-understanding partners and spouses for obvious reason, though I have some solutions in my sleeves

Failing in examinations or getting less marks in examinations may be short-term or long-term or both types of frustrations depending upon the person concern.

I cannot suggest any magic formula to avoid frustration. But I am trying to suggest few when one actually may be able to avoid frustration.

Let us discuss the short term frustration that I have cited in my earlier sub-chapter. You can reduce your anxiety and frustrations by following few simple steps.

Take few long breathe so that your lung is full of apparently fresh air.

Then ask this simple question to yourself, 'am I going to lose my job if I do not reach the meeting in time?' Most likely you will get a negative answer. Then ask the second question, 'will my boss scold me?' Most likely, this time you are going to get an affirmative answer. You should then remember what a senior must have told to you when you had joined into a service for the first time, if none has said to you earlier, please keep in mind for the rest of your life what I am going to say to you now. You are getting 50% of your salary for getting regular scolding from your boss. The next 30% of salary you are getting for scolding you subordinates. The rest 20% of your salary for getting the job and for coming to the office in time. If however, if you do not have any subordinate to scold then you can add that part of salary also in the first category. For work? Who cares for work in an office? On utilization front, the amount what you are going to get as your salary, is for looking after your family without any kind of gratification etc. Again you may ask me another question, 'if I cannot touch my salary, how I shall survive?' My answer for that would be, 'Your family will not allow you to die so easily and therefore, they will give you free food for your mere survival. However, if you are smart enough, you can keep increment arrears, bonus, travelling allowance etc. hiding from your hawk eyed spouse.' I am sure, you are not happy with my pessimistic answers. But please remember, only snake venom is the only medicine for a snake bite.

In the second case, you have to forget about the meeting at the tenth floor for the time being but you have to concentrate on the beautiful faces of the opposite sex (if however, you have no other orientation) entering into the lift. If you are connoisseur of beauty, you can enjoy the beauty of backside of the opposite sex as well of the outgoing visitors of your lift (dirty advices?). I know, you are actually doing that for the last thirty odd years.

Before we try to find out some workable solutions, we must try to understand why we become frustrated.

Basically two reasons of our frustration: First of all, we achieve less than our own expectations or expectations of our near and dear ones. Corollary to this reason, when we see less capable persons are more successful than us because of not having equal opportunity for you or for your near and dear ones. Your level of frustrations goes towards north, when a known person, having less opportunity is holding better position than you because of his own talent and endeavors. Second reason of our frustration is borne out of expectations from others on whom we have no control. A file is not cleared by your boss may be an example of the second type of reasons of frustration. Similar is the case when your son is not getting a job or a bride where you have little or no control of the situation.

However, if you closely examine both the causes of frustrations you will find a common cause from which both the causes are sprouted. That is nothing but our own selfishness to make us happy at the cost of someone else. It is human nature, we can only see who are standing before us and we never look back how many persons are standing behind us. If you can look back, I am sure at least fifty percent of your frustrations will be over.

Let me share one of my experiences while waiting for a city bus in the early nineties at Central Secretariat bus stand. A young boy of IIT Delhi joined me after five minutes of my waiting for a bus to Delhi University. As a talkative person, I initiated a conversation after standing another five minutes together at the bus stand. When he came to know that I was a Government Servant, he remarked indirectly accusing me, 'Delhi is a horrible place to live in. There is no administration. You see, we have to wait for a bus so long? Probably nowhere in the world has a worse city bus service than Delhi?'

With a smile I asked, 'Probably you have visited many cities of the world as well as the country side of our own country. Unfortunately, I have not visited abroad and many places of our own country.'

Sensing some verbal retaliation from me, he hesitantly said, 'No I have also not visited any other country. As a matter of fact, I have not visited any other city other than Mumbai.'

'What about any other state?'

'No sir, I have not.'

'Do you know, there is a state in India called Arunachal Pradesh situated in the North Eastern part of our country?' I asked him. He kept mum. Then I said, 'In that state and in some other states of North East, if you miss a bus, for the next bus you have to wait for a week or even for a month. Alternatively, you have to walk down for two days in a hilly track.' He did not say anything till bus arrived after five minutes.

We are frustrated because we expect from the other side much more compared to our brothers and sisters who are actually worse off than us and practically getting nothing compared to us. If you think about for them for a while your frustration level will come down considerably automatically.

There is another common frustration point about our income, 'my income is less than the income of others'. Is it true? In most of the cases, it is not true. But again, we see the wealthier people standing before us and forget to look back to the hungry mouths behind us crying for a single meal in a day.

When my children complain about load shedding for half an hour or so in the summer, I try to console them (in vain) that we did not have electric connection at my ancestral home till I passed out my graduation. I told them another fact that there was no fan in our hostel

(Hostels of Cotton College-the oldest and the best college of Assam at that time) till 1978. Incidentally, I joined Cotton College in 1976 as a higher secondary student.

I have experienced, the more facilities you are enjoying, the more chance of getting frustrated in your life.

Always remember, frustration is also a part of modern life. The moment you get up from bed you are exposed to some sorts of frustration. Suppose you are a youngster, the moment you get up, you will get some sermons from your mother or father or from elder brother or elder sister. You will find some of them are very irritating. Not coming to their expectations may itself be a very frustrating part of your life.

As a youngster of fifteen, you may have love in your eyes for someone. You do not know the mind of your loved one, then you become a frustrated one. Your frustration may increase when your relatively boring friend has already been able to win the heart of a gorgeous girl of your class.

As a youth of twenty five, you may be frustrated because you have not been able to crack an examination which will give an opportunity to clinch a good job.

After getting a job will not guarantee that you will be free from frustration. Similarly, even after your son gets a good job and your daughter's marriage to a good young man, do not guarantee to make you free from frustration.

Therefore, frustration whether it is short-term or long-term will not leave you alone till you leave this earth forever. Then why do you worry about your frustration? Try to love your frustration like your spouse as a necessary evil of your life. I am sure, with the above sentence, I have thrown a stone to a hornet's nest. But believe me that may be a good way to deal with your frustration.

I found many officers complain about their juniors of not being respectful for their seniors, particularly after retirement. Normally, while complaining they forget to ask one question to themselves, did they behave well with the juniors when they were in the helm of affairs? Did they love the juniors at par with their own children when their subordinates are of their children's age? In most of the cases you will get a negative answer. I am not saying that empathic boss will garner respect from all concerned always. But definitely chances are high for those bosses to get respect after their retirement. At least, I have not heard any complaining voices against the juniors from my empathic elderly colleagues even after their retirement.

I shall share with you another example where an old lady tried to commit suicide because of frustration. Why she was frustrated? Whether her children are not properly settled? Are they not providing shelter and food to her? No. She is blessed with all the earthly comfort. Her son is a senior officer in Government and daughters are also married to persons occupying positions in the society. Even her grandchildren are also doing well in their life. Her only complaint is that nobody has any time for her. Did she have time for any elderly person when she was young and energetic? As I know the old lady for a pretty long time and I know her as a lady who was only concerned about herself and her nucleus family. Her children saw her like that only and therefore they think providing food and shelter are enough for an old lady. In her young days she was not empathic for elderly family members of her husband's family as well as her own parents. But after death of her husband, being alone she was expecting all sympathy and empathy from her children and daughter in law. Many, those who did not know about the past of the lady and those who ignored the past even after knowing her past, blamed the daughter in law for the drastic step taken by the old lady. Somehow, I could not blame the daughter in law.

My suggestion for those who are frustrated about the present situation what I have explained above, please do not expect anything extra in your life what you had given to others. Even if you had done many good things to your elderly when you were young, please do not expect anything in return. Then only your frustration level will be always low, even then if you are frustrated sometimes, your frustration level will be well under control.

If you want to kill frustration, try to be free from all the negative thoughts. It is always easier said than done. We can put forward this suggestion very easily, but can we follow that in our own daily lives? Probably it will be empathic no from all of you. But what is the harm, if we try to make ourselves free from negative thoughts?

Finally, I am suggesting a single liner for your consideration to reduce your degree of frustrations.

Always thank God in the morning for what you are having till yesterday and in the evening tell yourself, in the whole day, you have done something for you, for your family, for the society you are living in, your country and above all, for all the living and non-living things on the mother earth, as per the best of your ability and understanding. I think your frustration will be lessen by a major portion. Further, if you can eradicate any expectation from others, you can make yourself free from 99% of your frustration.

My humble request to all of you to try my one liner for the next one month and see the result. Hope this one liner will reduce your frustration level considerably leading to a healthy and prosperous life.

Chapter: 62

Only For Your Happy Life

We are unhappy because we are not thankful to the Almighty what He has given to us without asking from Him.

You roll your eyes, you will find a good number of people around you who are either physically weaker than you or financially weaker than you or less intelligent than you. Have you ever thank God for making you healthier, financially stronger and more intelligent than many of the fellows surrounding you? If you do that, you will always be happy, otherwise not. To be happy or not to be, it is in your hand. Take your decision today and start smiling right now!

The following chapters may enlighten you, why we are unhappy and how we can overcome our unhappiness by some positive thinking.

You Are Unhappy Because You Are Not Thankful

In one of my visits to Guwahati, I met my old friend Dr. Subham. At present he is one of the leading Psychiatrist of Assam. When I went to his chamber, he told me to sit at his personal chamber so that he can finish his talk with a very young and handsome patient.

After five-ten minutes he came to his personal chamber and told me, 'Sorry, I am keeping you waiting for a long time. Hope you do not mind for that as you understand that, my job and patients are different from other doctors. This particular boy has a specific problem. He does not want to marry, fearing that his partner will not be happy with him.'

'Why?'

'This is not a very uncommon problem. Every man and woman has this fear before his/her marriage. However, the fear may be different for different person. For example, it may be due to financial, social, physical and sometimes, even for some unknown reasons. Financial reasons are the most common among males whereas it is uncommon among the females. However, physical reasons are not uncommon among both the sex. But a person seldom spells out about physical problems in public. Only a few highly educated people are coming to us for solution of physical problems. This particular boy is also from a very reputed family and he is presently working as an executive in a reputed public sector manufacturing company. His parents found a very beautiful girl from a very good family for him. The boy has nothing against the girl. But he does not want to marry her fearing that he will not be able to make her happy physically.' Subham paused for minute.

'Is he impotent?' I asked.

'No, but he has a feeling that his genital is not sufficiently big enough to satisfy a girl?' Dr. Subham told with a sigh. Dr. Subham's face became visibly looked sad. 'Initially, I have not told you that, unfortunately, he is my elder brother's son.'

A rare silence descended into the room. For some time, no one of us dare to break the silence.

Finally, Subham broke the silence, 'When he was young, as happens to many male children, his genital was relatively small and for that his peers used to make fun of him. But as a doctor, I know, after attaining adolescence, it grows to normal size. But some of the children cannot forget those blues of early life and mentally became upset about that and cannot cope up normal sexual life.'

'How one can come out of that psychological problem?' I asked.

'Through counselling. That is, exactly what I am doing with my nephew.' He paused for a moment. Then he explained me as a doctor.

'We try to convince them with two basic arguments: First, he does not have the smallest genital in the world. On the other hand, nobody cannot claim he has the largest one. Number two, to make your wife happy, sex is one of the factors as important as any other factors, like financial stability, mutual respect, understanding of each other's problem and above all, true love for each other. I asked them to give me one example in the world, where a mother loves the neighbor's son more than her own son, despite of knowing that her son is inferior in all accounts, compared to the son of her neighbor. Why? That is because, she loves her son no matter how good he is. A wife or a husband is a compact package which may include sex as an important component, but not the one and only component. Finally, we ask them a question, are you going to select your bride on the basis of the size of her breasts?'

'How long it will take?'

'Response from him is very good. It may be because, he is very close to me emotionally. But for unknown person, due to inherent inhibition it may take little longer. Faith on the doctor also matters.'

In the meantime tea was served. I tried to discuss some other things not related to his professional life nor mine. But Subham was no mood to finish his topic. He started a new case which is much more acute and damaging. It was about a very rich self-made man, Mr. Ardhendu Singh.

Mr. Ardhendu Singh, second son of the parents, was born to a middle-class family in the early 60s in a small village of Assam.

In due course of time, he became a very successful businessman without any family lineage in business. Without permission of his parents, he married to a lovely girl. After one year of marriage, he was blessed with twins, one son and a daughter. He is a good husband and a very good father who fulfils all the earthly demands of his wife and children. In the meantime, he had constructed a huge palatial building, bought two-three luxury cars, and established few factories. By the time, he had earned sufficient money not only to visit abroad on business tours but also capable of affording leisure tours abroad with or without family.

With all these good things, unfortunately he has been suffering from a major psychological problem from his early childhood. Nobody knew about it; including his parents and his loving and understanding wife. He does not want to discuss about the problem with anyone including doctor till recently. Instead, he tried to find a solution to his problem, through his own innovation, he wanted to discuss the matter only with unknown persons.

To implement his thoughts to experiments, he visited one brothel in Mumbai. Instead of having sex with sex worker, he asked her whether, his genital was sufficiently big enough to satisfy a lady. The perplexed sex worker said, 'it is a normal sized organ to satisfy any lady.' He was so happy to hear the answer, he gave few more bucks to the whore, over and above her due rates. He left the place without doing anything with the whore.

But after few days, a new thought had cropped up in his head, 'Was the prostitute lying to satisfy his ego and to get a tip for her good words?'

This wild thought engulfed his head, mind and entire thinking process. He lost a few nights' sleep. Then, finally he decided to ask the same question to another sex worker.

During a business tour in another city, he called a call girl to his hotel room and asked the same question. The girl was very beautiful and her voice was also very beautiful. With her beautiful voice assured him that, he is perfectly alright and looked for a good session. But Ardhendu did not want to cheat his wife and thanked the girl and let her go without any further talk.

For few days he was very happy.

But alas! The same haunting question had taken over him. During next twenty odd years he travelled entire world, from one continent to another, spending a lot of money. His odyssey is to find only one simple answer, 'Whether he is capable of satisfying his partner with the size he has?'

No brothel was unvisited by this man across the globe in the last twenty odd years. He started this voyage from Delhi to Lucknow, Patna to Kolkata, Mumbai to Pune, Bangkok to Pataya in Thailand, Netherlands to France, Australia to New Zealand, New York to Rio and so on. Everywhere he got the same answer, 'it is sufficiently large enough to satisfy any lady.'

But still he is not satisfied, because once he heard his father was confiding to his uncle that, his son had a very small instrument, unlikely to be a real man.

Tired of those experiments and due to guilty feeling, one day he confided his mental agony to his wife along with all his misadventures. After, overcoming initial shock, she cried for a long time. Then she got herself composed and discussed the whole matter as a very good friend of him. She comforted her emotionally drained husband and advised him to meet a doctor.

Finally, this man along with his wife, landed at Subham's clinic. Now he is under treatment, but he will take much longer time compared to other patients due to his age and dogmatic nature. Subham is sure, he will also come out from his shell and live a normal life in due course of time.

When he finished his second case, I asked him a pertinent question. 'Does any lady is suffering from similar problem.'

'Yes, some of the ladies are concerned about their size of breasts and hips. Unlike the size of genital of a male, size of breasts and hips are visible. To overcome the inferiority-complex many ladies are using padded bra or cushions for hips. But psychologically, ladies are stronger than men at least on this account. Therefore, they will not fear for a marriage on the basis of the size of their breasts or hips.'

He paused for a moment and with a grin he said, 'No lady has any psychological problem about size of her genital. Why do you know?'

'They do not have a visible size as such.' I said.

'Do you drink cold drink etc.?'

'Is it a question to be asked?'

'All the caps are of same size, irrespective of the bottle size, whether it is two litre bottle or 200 ml bottle. Ha ha ha.'

Then Shubham offered a cold drink to me with a twinkle in his eyes.

Actually, You Are Not the Shortest

What is your height? This question may be traumatic for many of us. Even if you are above National average, the moment you see a taller person standing before you, you may have a feeling, 'Wow, what a height he has! Why I am not that tall?'

Whenever, we compare ourselves, we always compare with a better placed person on that particular indicator and feel little (sometimes disturbingly more) depressed. How to avoid this inferiority complex.

Again, take the case of height. My younger daughter sometimes feels her height is not good enough, because she is shorter than her elder sister and another cousin. But she forgets that she is taller than ninety-seven percent of Indian ladies with a height of 5 feet four inches. Her somewhat inferiority complex stems up because her sister's height is five feet five and her cousin's height is five feet seven inches.

If you ask me, am I happy with my own height at 5-10, my reply is a 'no'. I would be happier if my height would have been six plus. Being a statistician I know Indian males' average height is less than my younger daughter's height. Then why I am not happy with my own height? But had I been a seven-foot-tall person, would I be happy? Perhaps not. I know, in that case, I would be an odd-looking person in my country. So, what is the perfect height? It is a million-dollar question and perhaps none has the all satisfying answer.

A lady of twenty-five asked me a very awkward question very recently. 'Sir, when you were young, many girls must had been mad after you!'

'Why?'

'Because of your height.'

I was little bit disappointed. No girl had approached me for my height in my youthful days. I was far disappointed as she did not praise my intelligence or eloquence etc. However, I thanked her for her compliments on my height.

Has my height helped in my life? Exactly I cannot remember if I got any benefit because of my height or otherwise. No doubt, I am happy to see shorter people around me and I am feeling uncomfortable when many taller people are surrounding me; even though I know world's most powerful men are not necessarily taller than I.

What was my preference for a girl as a lover or wife before my marriage? She should be polite, educated, from a good family and cute (not necessarily beautiful). Height-weight, large small actually did not figure in my liking and disliking. I always dislike a girl who was laud in her behavior and tastes. Finally, what I got a different story altogether.

I have many close friends who are taller than I and probably equal number of friends who are shorter than I. So, height has never been a criterion for my friendship or love with someone. Then why we are finicky about our own height? After all you are not the shortest or tallest person of the world. If, however, you are, you are a celebrity and therefore you should be more than happy in your life!

Darling, You Do Not Have the Smallest Breast

For a man height is a major concern and for a girl size of the breast may be a major concern for developing or maintaining self-esteem. Deliberately I am not mentioning about the size of a dick for a man, as a major concern, because you seldom get a chance to show your dick to an unknown gorgeous lady, As I have already mentioned, if the lady before whom you had to be naked is your mother or sister (up to a particular age) and lover (or wife), she does not care about the size of your dick. All those ladies who love you as a son, brother or lover or husband, they love you irrespective of your look, physical shortcomings or beauty.

Same thing happens for a girl for her father and brothers. She is not loved by these persons due to her beauty or otherwise. Even a lover and a husband do not love a lady on physical beauty or shortcoming for a long time. The two categories of people (husbands and lover) take you as composite package with many qualities even though first attraction may come from physical beauty. So far, I have not come across a single male who confessed before me that he fell in love with a girl because of the size of her breasts.

Then why a lady is worried for the size of her breasts? Liking of general public of a particular community for the size of breasts may also differ from another community. This particular piece of knowledge is acquired by me very recently only when a junior officer from a particular state said, 'Sir, we (he mentioned about his region comprising few states of India) do not like the large breasts of ladies of--(another region). We like our ladies with moderate size of breasts.' Then why you are depressed for not impressing the persons by your outer look who actually do not matter in your life?

Many may criticize me for looking a girl as a commodity. But honestly, that is not my intention. My intention of writing about size of the breast is to tell that size of breast does not matter for true love from someone who matters to you. It is exactly similar to the height of a male for his loved ones. Then why your self-esteem goes down for only the size of your breast? Enjoy whatever the size of your breast, after all, it is also a God's gift to you to serve your child as a mother what no father in this world can do.

Actually, You Are Not the Poorest

'Are you poor or rich?'

Whenever I ask this question while taking class to the middle level officers in different places, most of the officers use to say 'We are poor' and few use to keep mum to see my reaction.

I use to say them, 'I am going to make you richer, without giving a single penny to you today!'

It all started when my wife used to tell me always that 'we do not have money.' I started pondering, 'was she right in her assessment?'

Finally, I explained to her that we are rich, at least officially. I have been an income tax payer since I joined my service in 1985. In India, only 1.5 % people are paying Income Tax and I am richer than 98.5% population of India. If I add to this, another condition, the persons paying income tax more than a certain amount, I shall be in top 0.5% bracket, at least officially.

From that day onwards, without any addition to my income, I become a rich man in the eyes of my wife. Had I been happy along with her after that explanation? However that is again altogether a different story?

For the last few years whenever, I had to deliver a lecture to a group of officers in the twilight zone, I make them happy by infusing a feeling of richness among them.

I request all my fellow friends when they are facing some financial crisis, to think for those persons who are facing more financial hardship than them. I used to tell them, 'You are not the poorest person in the world. If you can manage only a square meal in a day there are crores of people, who cannot afford even a square meal in two days! If, however, if you can prove that you are the poorest person, some Bill Gates Foundation is always ready to help you!'

Actually, You Are Not the Most Deprived One

You must have experienced a feeling at least once in your life that you are a deprived one. This is not only true for a person, it is also true for a similarly placed group of persons. Even a country as a whole may think that way. I cannot say anything about group of persons or about a country, but I can say with 99% probability that you are not the most deprived one.

If you have sibling(s), you are bound to think at times that you are the most deprived child of your parents. But whether that is true or false, only few close relatives of yours may know. However, they will play politics out of it. Therefore, if you have only one sibling, it is better not to take your relatives into confidence, instead you confront your parents and talk straight to your parent to clear your doubt. If you have more than one siblings, I am sure only one of the siblings may be favorite of your parents due to some reasons, rest are equally placed with you. So, you should be happy that you are not the most deprived child of your parent.

In office, sometimes this feeling may haunt you. Here your best approach is to be happy by ignoring the deprivation feeling instead of trying to win over your boss. You can see in your office only a few are close to your boss, others are equally deprived of his/her favour like you. Remember one thing always, nothing is free in this world, even favour from your boss is not free. To get favours of your boss, you may have to work harder than rest of your peers, or you have to make your boss happy through other means, some of the other means may be morally correct and even some of them are immoral also. Therefore, one should be happy that you are not the most deprived employee working in your office or organization.

In society also, you may think sometimes that you are deprived by others in accessing to the common property/

facilities etc. Here also you will find only few are getting more access than you, rest are equally placed, or even there may be someone who may have less access than you. You can fight for your share of flesh, but never be depressed by thinking that you are deprived.

And most importantly, always thank God for whatever you have today; because many of your friends may not have those despite of their best efforts to acquire those things/ facilities etc.

The author was a Government servant and a man of vivid experiences derived from his official postings across the country, travels across India and numerous visits outside India. He is presently a retired person residing in the NCR.

List of published printed books

1. Random Thoughts through a Coloured Prism
2. Melody of Fragrance
3. Guilt: Gift of Winter Spring
4. How to become unpopular
5. Twenty-five Love Stories
6. Aparajita: Short Stories
7. Random Stories and Dilemma of an old man
8. Father's Choice: A Story of True Love
9. Three Goddesses and only one Rascal
10. Blessed One
11. Chandraprabha: The Iron Lady of Assam
11. Mula Gabharu: A Story of Extreme Valour and Patriotism
12. Blessed One: Part-II

13. Seuz Jonack (Assamese)
14. Meghar Arar Surya (Assamese)

List of ebooks:

1. Random Thoughts
2. Dilemma of a Young Mind
3. Funny Statistics and Serious Statisticians
4. Melody of Fragrance
5. Akhadya
6. Few Cities through the Lens of Hiranya Borah
7. Guilt: Gift of Winter Spring
8. Beautiful Ghost
9. Great Fighters: Grace of God
10. All Blurred
11. Putting kids to sleep
12. How to become unpopular
13. Soulmates
14. My grumpy Face
15. Love and Worries
16. Discussion of own Birth: A Taboo
17. Interview
18. Indecent Love Affairs
19. My Fair Lady
20. Waiting time
21. Two Stories
22. My Mother: Dashami Borah
23. Parineeta

24. Manorama
25. Unwanted
26. First Attempt
27. A father
28. The Portrait
29. Snapped Thread
30. Only He Knows
31. The Stupid Mother
32. The Same Old Story
33. The Old Scoundrel
34. Third Attempt
35. Some of my First Days and First Nights
36. Snubbed Twice
37. Have You Met the God
38. Frequent Flier
39. Messiah
40. Forgive and Forget
41. To Win or to lose
42. Call Girl
43. Beyond Blood Relation
44. Lady with a Black Car
45. My wife
46. Complete Woman
47. Diwali Gift
48. Romance with a Lady
49. Open Heart Surgery
50. My First Love

78. My Dear Sister
79. Selection While Waiting at the Airport
80. Oh Shit
81. Perverse
82. He Got Back His Wife
83. Beautiful Faces
84. Elder Sister
85. Good Morning
86. Prey
87. Pass on your Death to Someone Else
88. Colour of Holi
89. Why blame others
90. A Forbidden Issue
91. Hat-trick of Failures
92. Agony of Writers
93. Contrasts
94. Three Directors
95. An Unusual Love Affair
96. Birth Day
97. Do not Tell Anyone
98. Anupama
99. Late By Ten Years
100. Murder in a Foreign City
101. Strange Life
102. I love You Darling
103. Falsehood
104. Lady in the Park

105. Do Anything, I Shall comment

106. Professionalism

107. Art of Flirting

108. Are We Human

109. Old man and a Dog

110. Relation with Relatives

111. Sun and Cloud

112. My Second Lover

113. In a Meeting

114. Love at First Sight

115. A Psalm of Life

116. He Wants a Solution

117. Wings

118. Twenty-five Love Stories

119. Me and a Dozen Plus One Ghost Stories

120. Aparajita: Twenty Seven Short Stories

121. Nothing Official As Such

122. Illustrated Kids' Story

123. Hundred Ways to F & F your Popularity

124. Broken heart

125. Random Stories and Dilemma

126. A Phone Call

127. Revenge

128. Men, Women, Dogs and Bitches

129. Mera Pyar (Hindi)

130. Scandal

131. Anuradha

132. Looking for a wife at thirteen
133. Fenny My Hero
134. Frustration: How to Get Rid of It
135. Monster Father
136. Surprising Gift
137. Predator
138. Facts and Fiction
139. Father's Choice: A Story of True Love
140. Philamazan: The Last Princess
141. Daughter
142. Bleeding Heart
143. Missing Daughter
144. Satarupa: The brave Lady
145. Me and My Family
146. Life and Death
147. Winning Heart of her Husband
148. Love and War
149. Causes of Divorce
150. Accidental Meeting
151. Plane Crash-IV
152. Accidental Heroine
153. Two Brothers
154. A Princess
155. The Disgraced Princess
156. Sleeplessness
157. Two Friends
158. Waiting at a Bus Stop

159. Incarnation of a Modern Devil

160. The Gift

161. For A Mere Cup Of Tea

162. I Shall Wait For You

163. How Much I Earn

164. Purified with Own Blood

165. Ice Cool

166. Two Princesses

167. Luck and Chance

168. In a Rainy Night

169. Love at Last

170. Sacrifice

171. Three Goddesses and only one Rascal

172. Cold Blooded Murder

173. Murder Mysteries

174. Two Hearts One Beat

175. Chandra Prabha Saikiani

176. Beautiful Promises of the First Night

177. In the Highest Court of Justice (Drama)

178. My Teachers

179. An Incomplete Voyage of a Blessed One

180. Nothing Personal

181. Covid 19 Vs 2020 Wonderful Warriors

182. Communication skill

183. Covid Test

184. Sati Sadhani: The tragedy Queen of Assam

185. Subhra Shatadal: The Stunning Beauty

186. Mula Gabharu: The Ultimate Woman Warrior of Assam

187. Shoes with Wings

188. Riddles

189. Spiritual Wife Vs Real Wife

190. Abhayapuri: Pain and Ecstasy of a Young Man

Connect with him

Email: hbmb@rediffmail.com

Friend him on Facebook: hbmb@rediffmail.com

For Tweeter: hbmb@rediffmail.com

Website: Hiranya.com

Website: Hiranyaboraauthor.com

9 789356 686151

Printed by Libri Plureos GmbH in Hamburg,
Germany